The Power of the West
in the Economy of Grace

The Power of the West in the Economy of Grace

Reclaiming a Prophetic Stewardship
with an Ecosophic Worldview

ESKIL JONSSON

RESOURCE *Publications* • Eugene, Oregon

THE POWER OF THE WEST IN THE ECONOMY OF GRACE
Reclaiming a Prophetic Stewardship with an Ecosophic Worldview

Copyright © 2013 Eskil Jonsson. All rights reserved. Except for brief quotations in critical publications or reviews, no part of this book may be reproduced in any manner without prior written permission from the publisher. Write: Permissions, Wipf and Stock Publishers, 199 W. 8th Ave., Suite 3, Eugene, OR 97401.

Resource Publications
An Imprint of Wipf and Stock Publishers
199 W. 8th Ave., Suite 3
Eugene, OR 97401

www.wipfandstock.com

ISBN 13: 978-1-62032-909-2

All scripture quotations, unless otherwise indicated, are taken from the Holy Bible, New International Version®, NIV®. Copyright ©1973, 1978, 1984 by Biblica, Inc.™ Used by permission of Zondervan. All rights reserved worldwide.

Contents

Preface / vii
Introduction / 1

1 The Belief in Modern Rationality and the Economy of Grace / 11
2 The Loss of a Prophetic and Ecumenical Identity / 28
3 Outrationalization of the Moral Impulse / 38
4 The Critique against Globalization of Modern Economics / 48
5 Institutionalization of Religion / 59
6 The Sacralized Economy / 68
7 Market Orientation of Religion / 79
8 Towards an Ecosophic Economy / 86
9 The Reason for Faith in Modern Societies / 97
10 Peace and Justice in the Mysteries of Faith / 104
11 Concluding Analysis / 113

Bibliography / 137

Preface

My educational background is primarily in business management and economics, but I have served in international church and ecumenical bodies in different cultural contexts, and been involved in peace research and the promotion of social, spiritual and economic development. I have also made interdisciplinary studies that has involved ecological economy, theology, ethics, sociology and politics. My experience then is that rootcauses of conflicts are often related to the disintegration of modern and traditional cultures, which also involves religion, power, ethnicity etc.

"The Power of the West in the Economy of Grace" gives a critical perspective on the globalisation Western institutional structure of religion, economy and politics, which are dominated by an anthropocentric and vertical perspective where the rest of the world has been treated as an object for exploration and domination. It is then often assumed in business and politics that the culture of modernisation, progress and economic growth should still be the only solution for peace and sustainable development. The Economy of Grace on the other hand refers to ecumenical and ecological philosophies, which see spiritual, human and natural resources and knowledge as gifts of grace to be shared for the benefit of all.

The received view at least in the West is then that the sacred and profane spheres of society such as faith and economy or religion and science are two separate spheres of thought. In this study I want to show that the ecumenical and prophetic stewardship concept, also rooted in the Greek concept of *oikos*, should be reclaimed in order to promote a culturally integrated world with peace and justice.

Preface

It appears also that the prophetic stewardship concept has been largely lost since the Constantinian age in the 4th century, when Christendom became a state religion.

With the stewardship perspective I will show how the modern disintegration of religion and politics, according to the Lutheran doctrine of "the two-kingdom government" have given theological legitimacy to church and state power and the separation between "creation and salvation" as well. Therefore the prophetic stewardship concept needs to be reclaimed in order to reflect the holistic and prophetic mission of the church.

Finally I would like to take the opportunity and thank all those who have provided support and comments on different parts of the manuscript both at Uppsala University and elsewhere. In particular I have to mention Prof Sven-Erik Brodd, Prof Carl-Henric Grenholm, Prof em. Peter Söderbaum, Prof Mehari Gebre-Medhin, Uppsala and Prof William T. Cavanaugh at DePaul University, Chicago. They have kindly provided much valuable support and inspiration for my research, but I do of course take the sole responsibility myself for what is now presented. I am very grateful to my wife Anita and the family who have given me constant support during the writing.

Let me finally express my appreciation to Wipf and Stock Publishers who have kindly offered to publish this book.

Eskil Jonsson
Uppsala, Sweden
June 2013

Introduction

THE POWER OF THE WEST IN THE ECONOMY OF GRACE

IN WESTERN AND MODERNIZING societies it is often argued by mainstream politicians and the business community that globalization, with its belief in rationality, economic growth, and competition in a free market, is a necessary precondition for peace and sustainable development. On the other hand, we can also notice how the pressure for economic growth and progress is a threat against social, cultural, or ecological concerns. Typical of Western globalization of modernity and growth appears to be a lack of awareness that economy has originally been about stewardship of common resources in a household, where the members are mutually dependent for their livelihood. However, Western politics and markets still behave as if human and natural resources were largely unlimited and the domination of modern forces over traditional cultures and religions is commonly taken more or less for granted.

The classical understanding of stewardship is to a great extent rooted in a religious and traditional culture. As a result of modernization and secularization it has been narrowed and replaced with the popular concept of management and free market economics. This is also due to the pressure from market competition, economic growth, financial management, and control in order to accumulate necessary financial resources needed for modern development and welfare (and warfare in order to secure power and economic growth).

As a remedy to the disintegrating impact of globalisation with increasing power concentration, competition, conflicts or injustices

The Power of the West in the Economy of Grace

I will in this book demonstrate some challenges of an ecumenical stewardship with a mutual responsibility. It is then believed that an ecumenical church and religion, as a sign of peace, justice and unity, should have an important prophetic role in the world. In contrast to a Western and anthropocentric view I seek support here from theological and ecological philosophies which stress the unity of Spirit, Humanity and Nature. This will be further explained in the following.[1]

WESTERN GLOBALIZATION

The impact of Western globalization, with pressures for privatization and modern market orientation on a global scale, has recently been illustrated very dramatically after the fall of the Berlin wall and the intervention from the West into many states in the East as well as the South. Naomi Klein has described an "economy of war" in her book *The Shock Doctrine* and how, for instance, poor workers, women, and rural populations have been marginalized. The expansion of the European Union (EU) into the East has also resulted into downsizings of social costs and privatization of public assets in order to boost world economic growth.

Typical of Western globalization and its belief in economic rationality, growth and progress has for a long time also been the universal spread of highly elaborate institutional structures in order to steer management, administration, staff, and workers. Much of these institutional systems are universally standardized according to Western culture, but not well adapted to the local identity, culture, or religion. The globalization of the modern market economics relies increasingly on the self-interest of the individual, seen as a "consumer," with little attention to common social responsibilities.[2]

Quite recently, we have also been made aware that accelerated industrial and economic growth will cause serious threats to the climate and other common ecological concerns. It is then believed

---

1. See Giddens, *The Consequences of Modernity*; Meyer, "Institutionalized Organizations"; Baumann, *Postmodern Ethics*; and Jonsson, *Narrow Management*.

2. Scott, *Institutional Environments*.

Introduction

the rich and powerful North has a huge ecological debt to poor countries in the South and to coming generations as well, which is a serious threat to peace and justice. This is widely seen as an exploitation of common natural resources, which will affect coming generations as well. On top of that, the huge investments made for modern development and economic growth mostly in urban areas tend to create increasing income gaps and social injustice, although the educated and employed middle class may benefit economically. The military expenditures increase in many Western nations not least in order to secure access to natural resources in the East and the South. This has also contributed to severe debt crises, which may threaten democracy, economic justice, and world peace. The lack of coordinated efforts to deal with such common social and ecological threats has raised a lot of critique against the modern economic systems and power structures of the West.

GLOBALIZATION OF CONFLICTS

In recent history and particularly during the twentieth century, we have seen how world conflicts have centered around capitalism or communism, between the United States and the Soviet Union, and between North and South.

In the new era of globalization, we can see how a new conflict pattern emerges, which is a threat to world peace and unity. The new political understanding of conflicts are by the super powers often described as "intrastate" between different ethnic or cultural identities. The conflicts may often be provoked by the competition for power over minerals and energy resources much because of Western interests in the rest of the world.

The events after the September 11, 2001 attacks on the US have been explained as a "war on terror" or even as "clashes between civilizations."[3] These clashes could, on the other hand, be described as a way to get religious or cultural legitimacy for the political and economic powers in conflict: traditional religious/feudal authorities against modern religious and modern liberal economy of the

3. Huntington, *The Clash of Civilizations*.

West. Other experts have explained how the impact from Western exploitation of oil in Arab countries has caused a lot of opposition from local people and authorities.[4]

Local and religious communities have traditionally been able to live together in peace for many years, but with the rapidly increasing Western and economic globalization, new conflicts emerge between central authorities and "illegal combatants" in traditional cultures and along new war fronts. During the last few decades, we have also seen how people from the new frontiers of conflict have to take refuge in the West, but are not easily getting political asylum there.

As we shall demonstrate in the following Western churches, voluntary and aid agencies have played a significant role in the Western support for national development, education, and economy, which have created a lot of fragmentation and cultural conflicts between the modern West and the traditional South.

This happens despite the fact that the prophetic identity of the church, and religion, is about peace, love, and unity. I will therefore depart from a critical perspective on the institutional and economic power of the modern West in an attempt to demonstrate how faith communities can strengthen their prophetic identity when applying the powerful model of stewardship.

GLOBALIZATION AND THE WESTERN CHURCH

In a brief historical overview of the expansion of the Western church, I will highlight the background to the legitimating role that religion has played for the power of the state and the institutional structure in society at large. Lucius Boraks concludes in his *Religions of the West* that great schisms developed in the past between Eastern religions and the Western church, which was due to "cultural, geographical, and linguistic differences" in the various political contexts.[5]

We can find the origin of Western religions already in the Old Testament history of the Jewish people, when they were seen as the people of God, called as slaves out of Egypt to be set free in the promised land of Israel. The Old Testament prophets were also

4. Labévière, *Dollars for Terror*.
5. Boraks, *Religions of the West*.

known for their prophetic critique against slavery and other injustices and oppressions of the people. The different faiths of Judaism, Christianity, and Islam are also rooted in this same religious tradition and peace should be their core identity as manifested in their words of daily greeting (*shalom*, *peace*, and *salam* respectively).

The vision of a prophetic and united church as a sign of peace in the world was envisioned in the New Testament by Jesus and his apostles, who preached the gospel of grace and love for all, regardless of religious affiliation, nationality, and culture. Local communities of believers were also established in order to bring this message of peace, unity, and justice to the world, first in Jerusalem and then in the Near East and Asia Minor. In Apostle Paul's first letter to the Corinthians in Asia Minor, he writes that they should identify themselves as "stewards of the mysteries of grace." He also described the unity as a "human body with different but interdependent limbs," where all members had a unique role to play in order to manifest unity and peace in the world. Later the followers, called Christians, were, however, brutally persecuted as they refused to worship the Roman emperor. They consisted largely of slaves and poor who were not well recognized in the society. It should, of course, also be underlined that women, to a greater extent than men, were among the followers, rather than men who totally dominated the political and religious authorities, which were in strong opposition to the radical message of peace and justice.

In the fourth century, however, they received protection from the emperor, Constantine I, whose mother was a Christian. A Roman church became later established with more formal and rigid hierarchical structures, and received legitimacy and support as a state religion. Several ecumenical councils were held in order to institute a united doctrine and laws to be followed, and the emperor was the one to oversee that the laws of the state and the religious doctrines were enforced. However, over a long period—up to the twelfth century—great schisms developed between churches in the East (Constantinople) and the West (Rome). Several crusades from the Roman Empire and church towards the East finally led to a complete separation and the formation of an independent Orthodox Church. It was also believed this weakened the Roman Empire, and it could be a major reason why Islam eventually became the dominant religion in the Near East and Asia Minor after brutal holy wars between the Roman Empire and Eastern cultures and religions. As a result of this schism the Roman Catholic Church was established in the West where Latin was the dominant language, separately from the Orthodox Church, where Greek was the main language.

Since the beginning of the Enlightenment period in the sixteenth century and the Lutheran Reformation period, the evangelical, Protestant, or Reformed churches were established in Northern Europe as a protest to the pope in Rome. This was mainly due to the sale of indulgences in order to finance St. Peters cathedral, widespread corruption, as well as major doctrinal differences. In Sweden for instance, King Gustav Vasa accepted a Lutheran state church in the sixteenth century, and the Roman Catholic Church was to be abolished. The national Lutheran Church also gave strong support for a modern nation state with modern science, education, and social welfare. With the rising belief in liberalization and democracy around the turn of the twentieth century mission, organizations and other diaconal organizations were formed as self-governing bodies, constituted with their own institutions and doctrines. In particular, a pietistic awakening, with its roots in Protestantism and a growing liberalism, emphasized a personal and individual confession, which resulted also in many different free churches and mission associations. They also played an important role in giving legitimacy to privatization, capitalism, and business entrepreneurship as part of the support for modern development and welfare.

In *Transforming Mission*, Bosch gives a similar view about the institutional differentiation of the Western church from the Eastern church. He also gives a thorough account of the paradigm changes of the mission of the church from the early Christian period up to the present. I depend very much on his knowledge and views about the theological identity of the church and the mission to the world. It becomes clear that the outreach and expansion of mission organizations of the Protestant churches during the twentieth century comes in the wake of the Enlightenment period. He gives the main contours of the Enlightenment worldview where God is placed at the top of the power hierarchy. Then comes the church, the king, and the power of the people over animals, plants, and objects.⁶ What is happening in the twentieth century is a shift in missionary thinking towards an ecumenical paradigm. Mission is the "church-with-others"⁷ and he sees the church as a sign, sacrament, or instrument, where the local church is rediscovered. God is turning to the world and it is God's mission; mission is a quest for justice, and there is an increasing criticism against modern capitalism.⁸

When I later outline the meaning of stewardship as an "economy of grace" and a matter of mutual responsibility, it is in contrast to the Western worldview with its belief in rationality, progress, growth, and power referred to above. Bosch does not, however, say anything about religion or the people of God as stewards, although I see it to be congruent with the "emerging ecumenical paradigm of mission."⁹ This new ecumenical paradigm of mission should also be a contribution to the new ecological worldview that I will elaborate on later.

CHURCH, MISSION, AND DEVELOPMENT

The Western churches also became committed to foreign mission and social development in the East and the South during the nineteenth century, which, however, still reflected corresponding doctrinal differences. The concept of "development" assumed that traditional societies would be brought to a similar level of living standard as that of the West and they were therefore called "developing countries." Also, here cultural, geographical, and linguistic differences have played a role in the institutional differentiations, but even more the differences in local ethnicity have been used to create legitimacy for power and to get access to resources, which have threatened the identification within a united church.

The foreign missionaries from Western churches were pioneers for philanthropic work in what was later seen as "development." Already at the beginning of the nineteenth century, humanitarian

---

6. Bosch, *Transforming Mission*, 263.
7. Ibid., 368.
8. Ibid., 435.
9. Ibid., 368.

work, primary education, and healthcare for the poor and sick had been initiated by missionaries who were usually identifying themselves within the local and traditional culture. They were usually supported by mission friends, which was the result of an increased awakening in the West. Mission stations were established most often in places remote from urban centers and the work was integrated around preaching the gospel, feeding the hungry, and healing the sick. However, some of the stories about these interventions also tell us that they too were motivated by the desire to help the "uncivilized" people, who were stuck in "backwardness" rather than looking forward to modern civilization and development.

Later on local congregations were established and local staff was trained to do much of the work. Almost parallel to the decolonization in the new developing countries, national churches were formed, but there were also a lot of resistances from some of the European missions to hand over the responsibility to local leaders. Some of the mission organizations even felt that their identity as a mission organization would then be lost.

Particularly since the Second World War and then the development boom in the 1960s, there has been a major increase of modern development projects from the Western world into the newly formed nations in traditional cultures of the East and South. There was a strong belief in modernization among politicians, economists and state aid agencies, and large investments in modern urban and rural development projects as well as higher educational institutions were made. These would now lift the poor nations out of poverty and even become important producers of raw material to Western industries. The aid was now to be given towards a specific project with detailed goals and means, as the new and secular aid agencies were very reluctant to give any support for faith-based communities. Huge loans were also given to finance a multiplicity of investment projects, which, however, the young nations later on were not able to repay, as the economic growth was too slow or not well integrated within the local and traditional cultures. Much of the loans were also given, as there was a great need of the banks in the West to get a good return on the huge capital that in the 1970s had been deposited by rich oil countries from the Middle East.

Introduction

In many of the so-called "failing economies," structural adjustment programs (SAP) were now demanded from the World Bank and aid agencies in order to cut public expenditures and boost economic growth. What happened then was an emphasis on export commodities rather than local food production in order to bring foreign currency, which was needed in order to pay for loan repayments and imports for modern development. What also happened around the turn of the century was an increasing preference for business relations and market orientation rather than supporting the organization as a whole.[10]

In my previous working experiences as financial controller in church-related organizations between 1970 and 2004, and during my doctoral studies from 1992 to 1998 on the aid relations between Western and East African churches, I observed some conflicts and tensions, which seemed to be rooted in the differences between what has been described as modern and traditional identities. It was difficult both for the supporting bodies and also for the recipients of aid to integrate a multiplicity of bilateral and earmarked support within the local and united church. Huge funds could then be accumulated in some of the projects, which had become difficult to implement due to cultural conflicts, while other projects could not be implemented due to lack of funds for a specific project. The funding from foreign state aid agencies could be secured only on the condition that the secular development projects were separated from what was regarded as church-related projects. This was however, a problem for some of the church leaders who saw the total work of a united church as a holistic mission, including both social and spiritual matters. Another problem was of course that the Western aid as such also created a heavy dependence on foreign techniques and state funding, which made it difficult to raise support from local congregations of the church. The power of aid made real equality and economic justice unrealistic. Plans for self-support and integrated stewardship were worked out, but these plans could not be implemented, as it was easier to get access to large sums of aid from the West. The conclusion I reached was that management was too narrow and was dominated by belief in

10. Korten, *Alternatives to Economic Globalization*.

economic rationality and modernization. Additionally, Western aid agencies have increasingly preferred to designate their aid according to their own policies, which has made it difficult to maintain a united identity of a local church.[11]

CONCLUSION

The main conclusion I would like to make in this introduction is that the power and institutional structures of the West with the rise of the Roman Empire, the expansion of the Western Church, the Western Enlightenment, and the recent postmodern period of Western globalization created excessive divisions, conflicts, injustices, and fragmentation. This can also lead to a centralization of power and resources.

This introductory chapter indicates also that ecumenical, prophetic, or religious identity as signs of peace may be severely threatened through affiliations with the power of the state or the king. This was quite clear already in the fourth century when the Roman emperor Constantine I accepted Christendom as state religion. In a similar way I assume that the meaning and identity of stewardship has withered away ever since. It should therefore be important to critically analyze the institutional development with the Western economic systems and power structures from a new stewardship perspective that pays due attention to ecumenical, interreligious and multicultural responsibility as signs of peace, unity and justice.

In the next chapter I will show how the Western and egocentric worldview of globalization and modern economic rationality is also increasingly questioned due to the threat against social, cultural, or ecological sustainability. Many sociologists, ecologians, and religious scholars suggest a new ecological worldview that recognizes long-term sustainability with the integration of different social, cultural, and religious identities. I will therefore outline the essence of an ecosophic stewardship model, where spirit, humanity, and nature are all treated as a gifts of grace, and are seen as interdependent within a common identity and worldview.

---

11. Jonsson, *Narrow Management*.

1

The Belief in Modern Rationality and the Economy of Grace

I WILL HERE GIVE a brief theoretical explanation of the Western institutional systems with its belief in modern rationality, economic growth and progress, which can make it difficult to recognize spiritual, traditional, and even social and ecological philosophies. Therefore I will outline the model of stewardship as an "economy of grace," which can integrate the wider sphere of spirit and culture with human and natural resources. This will be done with particular reference to the prophetic and ecumenical identity of the church demonstrating peace and unity in the wider household of God.

MODERNITY AND DISEMBEDDEDNESS

The characteristics of modernity are described typically as a contrast to what is then seen as traditional. Anthony Giddens[1] says that modernity is generally characterized by disembedded social relations, and has developed from the Enlightenment period since the seventeenth century and the progress of the West. These relations are being lifted out of the social and cultural context, time, and space and modernity implies a strong belief in scientific knowledge,

1. Giddens, *The Consequences of Modernity*.

technological development, institutionalization, and economic progress over and against the traditional cultures and religions.

Since the beginning of the 1980s, it has been common to speak about postmodernity, a concept propounded by the French philosopher Michel Foucault and others. Within the economy and society, this is predominantly characterized by an increasing economic rationality with networking, privatization, competition, and market orientation. Advocates of the postmodern view describe the old modernity as typically hierarchical and top-down with a prison-like character, where detainees are controlled from above or from the outside with a panoptical perspective.

Gidden says, however, that postmodernity is more like a radicalized modernity or high modernity. It implies a shift from unified national political governance to a typical fragmentation of self-interests with little coordination in relation to overall identity, or purpose. Consequently, the power is located in the market system and is thus also disintegrated from the social and cultural context, not really being a part of the market system of buying and selling all sorts of goods and services.

I do not therefore see postmodernity as basically different from modernity. Like Giddens, I see globalization rather as a radicalization of modernity, which is the result of an expanding process of rationalization, and moves into a higher modernity when it is dominating the political, economic, and democratic power structures. Zygmunt Baumann applies a similar view when he talks about the "out-rationalization of the moral impulse" in his book *Postmodern Ethics*.[2]

INSTITUTIONAL-CULTURAL ANALYSIS

The analysis of how modern institutional structures and economic systems are formed, how they operate and change, and how they influence behavior in society has now become a major subject of inquiry in politics, sociology, and economics.

2. Baumann, *Postmodern Ethics*.

The Belief in Modern Rationality and the Economy of Grace

In religious sociology, Thomas F. O'Dea explained in 1961 how religious institutions face institutional dilemmas between the need for institutions, such as liturgy and sacraments to maintain or strengthen the mystery of faith and on the other side the problem of institutionalization of power. This is of course a problem that will increase also in the Western context, which stresses the belief in an instrumental rationality with the constitution of doctrines, confessions, laws, rules and regulations.

Meyer, as one of the most prominent authors in the new institutionalism stream of institutional analysis, argues that in the late nineteenth century most developed countries went through an organizational revolution as part of their modernization process.[3] Institutional systems in disparate sectors such as the economy, the political order, education, religion, etc., evolved to become formal organizations. The process was seen everywhere as progress and rationality was the focus—the controlled, unified mapping of human activity around purpose, segregated from the more irrational aspects of social life. New institutionalism writers of this cognitive stream base much of their arguments on Weber[4] and his well-known "rationalization processes," which he uses particularly in order to explain the legitimating of power and domination.

The meaning ascribed to *institutionalization* here makes it almost synonymous with rationalization processes, but there is a particular emphasis on the creation and diffusion of organizations, economic systems, structures, formal rules, etc., which implies a "differentiation between the institutionalized system and the life world" outside the system. The particular design of institutional and economic structures is then often not really very rational or purposive in relation to the overall identity, purpose, or strategy. According to new institutionalism writers, organizations derive their structural characteristics from the *rationalization* of a fragmented institutional resource environment, in order to get financial support or to justify their own authority.[5] This process has meant that organizational sys-

---

3. Meyer et al., *Institutional Structure*, 12–37.
4. Weber, *Economy and Society*.
5. Meyer and Rowan, "Institutionalized Organizations."

tems and processes reflect a differentiated environment embracing a diversity of rationalized institutional elements such as projects, functions, job-titles, processes, regulations, plans, budgets, etc.

The belief in institutional rationality thus creates fences around the institutionalized system, closing it off from the overall identity or from the local and cultural context for which the various institutions were established. As Meyer put it, "progress cannot be attained without specifying the boundaries within which progress is to occur." They add that even "equality is not attainable without a precise unitary definition of the entities that are to be equal and it compels a sharpened conception of the individual . . . the further rationalization is pushed, the more the individual (as an institutional category) must be enhanced and expanded."[6]

This means that processes of rationalization and institutionalization are likely to lead to disintegration from the "human beingness" of the individuals concerned. In this connection Meyer argues also that the content of the epithet "economic" has been expanded as nation states have proliferated: "Because modern polities are rationalized and monitories, it has become common to think of huge sectors of society as 'economic' although they have nothing to do with the commodity economy."[7]

Without going into detail, I think it is fair to say the establishment of the European Union financial institutions over the last decades can be taken as a good illustration of the expanding modern economic culture, which seems to work against the original purpose to maintain peace and unity. Leaders and ministerial staff are now very occupied in safeguarding the availability of funds for economic growth within Europe, while global economic injustice, poverty, climate threats, etc., outside the European union (EU) do not receive much attention. In the US, we have also seen how the demand for economic growth and the competition for power over energy resources needed for the growth causing a huge increase in national debt, internal political conflicts, as well as the world's highest military budget.

6. Meyer et al., *Institutional Structure*, 25–26.
7. Ibid., 44.

The Belief in Modern Rationality and the Economy of Grace

THE WESTERN EGOCENTRIC VIEW

Modern theories and strategies for development are described above as processes of rationalization, which are mostly based on a Western worldview of domination, growth, and disintegration in relation to what is called traditional cultures. Some management researchers say that these theories assume a Western "egocentric" view, where the human exploitation of natural resources from all over the world is taken more or less for granted. This worldview and philosophy of management is, however, now increasingly being questioned even in some of the leadership and organizational literature. They suggest therefore a new *eco-centric* paradigm. Purser, Park, and Montuori state in an article of *Academy of Management Review*:

> These epistemological conventions (modern management) are socially reproduced in organization science and management practice in their more contemporary anthropocentric forms: a disembodied form of technological knowing conjoined with an egocentric organizational orientation. Following this critique, the paradigmatic differences between anthropocentric and eco-centric approaches for dealing with issues related to the natural environment are discussed in what is referred to respectively as the environmental management and eco-centric responsibility paradigms. Our analysis suggests that corporate environmentalism and so-called "greening-business" approaches are grounded in the environmental management paradigm" . . . Environmental management approaches are incommensurable with the eco-centric responsibility paradigm.[8]

In a similar vein, Davis suggests a "stewardship theory of management." He states that in contrast to the *agency theory* of business management, assuming a conflict of interest between owners of capital and managers, the stewardship theory of management assumes a common interest and identity with relation to managers and the staff. In agency theory, hierarchical structures of

---

8. Purser, Park, and Montuori, "Limits to Anthropocentrism."

15

organization and financial benefits are continuously developed in order to steer the subordinates to direct the performance and efficiency of managers.[9]

There is an increasing realization also among social scientists, ethicists, and ecological experts that we need a new development theory, which pays greater attention to social and spiritual aspects that can support a sustainable development in poor countries.[10] Korten is of the opinion that neoclassical economic theories depart from business corporations and nations as the unit of analysis, rather than taking the local household and society (micro ecosystem) as the point of departure for the analysis.

Korten also states that the people have been alienated from the community, which is due to the modern dualism in the West, which separates human beings from nature. Dualism was an important reality for the Enlightenment philosopher René Descartes, whose thesis was that humans ruled over nature. Institutional authorities, to boost industrialization and over utilize natural resources, have then used this simple idea. A theory for sustainable development must therefore, they mean, be based on the conviction that humanity constitute a spiritual whole.

Elinor Ostrom from the United States, who received the Sveriges Riksbank Prize in Economic Sciences in 2009, has raised interest for mutual responsibility. Her book *Governing the Commons* demonstrated that resource management in the social economy involves a mutual cooperation in the formation of institutional structures, which was found to be more effective than conventional organizational theories suggest. She also states that it is important to apply a wider interdisciplinary framework and to take account of the social, ecological, and cultural context where institutionalization takes place.

What modern businessmen do not say much about, however, is that mutual cooperation has contributed greatly to growth and welfare in the past. It is even much older than the State and the business company and many other organizations we know

---

9. Davis, "Toward a Stewardship."
10. Korten, *The Post-Corporate World.*

The Belief in Modern Rationality and the Economy of Grace

of. Furthermore, the traditional cultures in most countries of the world, including the East and South, of course have institutions reflecting a culture of mutual responsibility and social integration. I will return to this later when describing the multicultural and multi-religious economy.

In Sweden for instance this communitarian form of local associations (*förening, gille, skrå*, etc.) consist of members who join with a purpose to serve the community. There was a great expansion in the early nineteenth century when many associations were formed as free churches, revival movements, labor unions, and cooperatives. It is also important to realize that these movements are the ones that have laid the foundation for much of the economic growth, social welfare, peace, and democracy.

What is very strange, however, is that education in modern economics is almost exclusively about public and business administration, which to a very large extent have their origin in the West. Modern economics and management inspired by Western universities have also been spread universally to most countries of the world. The keywords are: hierarchies, market competition, self interest, financial capital and economic growth, which however are not adapted to social and local identities and even less to the core identity of religion and the church.

TOWARDS AN ECO-SOPHIC WORLDVIEW

Some ecological philosophers argue now that modern Western worldviews have for too long assumed an anthropocentric or egocentric perspective, where the West is seen at the center of the world and views the rest of the world as an object for exploitation for its own benefit. In response to this, they argue in favor of an *ecosophic* worldview that integrates humanity, spirit, and nature. Each organism's own value and ecology is not just about nature, but about inter-human relations and social justice as well. Also the spiritual, cultural, and material matters, which in premodern ages had been seen as an integrated whole, now need to be reintegrated.[11]

---

11. See Bateson, *A Sacred Unity*; Skolimowski, *Ecological Humanism*.

According to Derek Wall, a prominent British green proponent, there are four pillars that define green politics: ecology, social justice, grassroots democracy, and nonviolence.[12] Social justice for instance was initially coined in the 1840s by moral theologians and rooted in the writings of St. Thomas Aquinas. Today all of these so-called "green pillars" are still central to many other theologians from various faith communities as well as green parties and civil rights movements, although various concepts have different nuances depending on the cultural context.

When reviewing the history of ecological philosophies it is interesting to find that the modern concepts of ecology with sustainability or green politics are all to some extent rooted in the original identity of economy as a household, where members are mutually dependent for their livelihood. However, in modern and Western interpretations of ecology, green economy, and sustainability it is common that it is limited to the natural environment. There are very few considerations of the ecological or economic debts that the Western civilization have in relation to the sustainability in the rest of the world.

STEWARDSHIP AS ECOLOGICAL HUMANISM WITH ST. FRANCIS

The ecosophic worldview I am referring to has perhaps best been explained as an ecological humanism. It stresses the interdependency between humanity, spirit, and nature, and underlines that all humans need to act together as *stewards* with a mutual responsibility in order to share the resources which are for the benefit of all.[13]

Skolimowski sees in the ministry of St. Francis a model for an ecological ethic based on empathy with all creation. We must see the connection between the healing of the earth and the healing of ourselves, he says. Values such as living simply, frugally, and responsibly must be brought to the fore. And, in the spirit of St.

---

12. Wall, *The Rise of the Green Left*.
13. Skolimowski, *Ecological Humanism*.

The Belief in Modern Rationality and the Economy of Grace

Francis, there can be no separation of ecology from issues of justice for the oppressed.

In short, ecological humanism is based on a new articulation of the world at large:

- It sees the world not as a place for pillage and plunder, an arena for gladiators, but as a sanctuary in which we temporarily dwell, and of which we must take the utmost care.
- It sees man not as an acquisitor and conquistador, but as a guardian and steward.
- It sees knowledge not as an instrument for the domination of nature, but ultimately as techniques for the refinement of the soul.
- It sees values not in pecuniary equivalents, but in intrinsic terms as a vehicle that contributes to a deeper understanding of people by people, and a deeper cohesion between people and the rest of creation.
- It sees all these above mentioned elements as a part of "new tactics for living."

In the following, I shall therefore further explain the philosophy of stewardship that is rooted in the original meaning of economy seen as a household, which contrasts with the modern economics of competition for power over resources now dominating the global market.

STEWARDSHIP AS AN ECONOMY OF GRACE

Basically, a nation, organization, and community or even the whole universe is according to the traditional *oikos* concept seen as a family or household where the different parts or members are mutually interdependent for their livelihood. The prophetic identity of the church and even the humanity as a whole is seen as a united body with interdependent limbs. This image signifies the common and core identity of the church to be a sign of grace, to manifest mutual solidarity, peace, and justice as a "moral community."[14]

The identity of a united and prophetic church is often explained as the body of Christ where all the limbs of the body have a unique role to manifest the grace of God. Ecumenical stewardship also implies different people acting as stewards of God in mutual solidarity with various spiritual and natural resources as signs of peace, mutual responsibility, and unity. The same image is also illustrated in the vertical axis of the holy cross that represents the relation between spirit and nature and the horizontal axis representing the identification with humanity. It manifests thus the integration of the sacred and the profane spheres of the world.

In the universal church, the sign of grace, unity, and peace is manifested in a symbolic way through the institution of sacraments in the church. The baptism, for instance, demonstrates the grace of God given to the individual person as well as the integration within the church as a community of believers. The sacrament of the Eucharist demonstrates the peace offered by Christ, mutual sharing, and love within the church and the global household.

A wider meaning of stewardship in the economy of grace is that every creature (humans, animals, and plants) can also be seen as stewards, as all have a specific role to play for the benefit of others as well. Thus, the essence of stewardship and a united church is *mutual responsibility* and *service* rather than a matter of law, formal authority, or direction from the top.

Among the early church fathers, in particular, the Greek concept of *oikonomia* (economy of grace) was important in understanding the comprehensiveness and integration that existed between different persons of the Trinity. However, it was on this point that doctrinal differences first developed. The Western churches maintained that the Trinity should be expressed as the Holy Spirit, the Father, and the Son while the Eastern churches wanted to stress the Holy Spirit, the Lord, and Life-Giver.[15]

The model of stewardship has in a modern American tradition been outlined as a servant-hood leadership, meaning that

---

14. Mudge, *The Church as a Moral Community*.
15. Meeks, *God the Economist*.

The Belief in Modern Rationality and the Economy of Grace

management is giving service and support rather than direction and control. Our model of an ecosophic stewardship (or ecocentric) is much more inclusive and stresses in the same way as Trinitarian stewardship the interdependence of spirit, humanity, and nature.

In recent decades several ecological philosophers, theologians, and even some management researchers have also highlighted the concept of stewardship as the open rationality commensurate with ecological humanism as well as eco-theological philosophy. This concept is rooted in the Greek word *oikonomia* (*oikos* for household or family and *nomos* meaning strategy, plan, or order). The strategy, leadership, or structure of stewardship departs from identity of the church, where unique gifts—human, spiritual, cultural, or natural—are seen as the grace of God to each and everybody, and should be shared freely for the benefit of all members of a household or community (economy of grace).[16]

Berry argues that we need to revisit the old concept of stewardship in order to understand the essence of mutual responsibility. Modern development after the Western Enlightenment had, however, created a rift between the sacred and the profane, contrary to the stewardship philosophy as well as the ecosophic worldview.

STEWARDSHIP AS IDENTIFICATION WITH OTHERS

The deeper meaning of identity and faith comes out in the Greek word *oikodomé*, which denotes identification with others (to be touched). In modern usage of the word, to be touched is associated with merely emotions and personal matters. Here it is manifested in the stewardship idea as identification within the wider social and cultural context. Service to and trust in others is therefore crucial for the meaning of stewardship here. Trust in modern institutional arrangements will therefore depend on the transparence of institutions in order to allow a mutual accountability. Stewardship assumes

---

16. See Brattgård, *God's Stewards*; Meeks, *God the Economist*; Long, *Divine Economy*; Nelson, *Economics as Religion*; Tanner, *Economy of Grace*; Berry, *God's Book of Works*; Atherton, *Transfiguring Capitalism*.

instead a trust in the steward's ability to manage according to overall and common identity and purpose. Credibility, reliance, and confidence are therefore central characteristics for a good steward. Changes in the modern usage of stewardship as management can show how trust instead is connected with detailed control systems, elaborate evaluations, contractual arrangements, and internal audit systems established by the management and owners of capital.

In order to understand the concept of stewardship in contrast to the exercise of power, it is necessary also to reflect comprehensively on the understanding of *self* and belonging within a community. Identity is therefore not just a matter of origin or individual character. It is defined in relation to the wider social and cultural context. Mutual responsibility and servant-hood requires responsibility to offer one's own gifts, talents, and resources both for personal development and for the benefit of the community at large. Credible stewardship implies that stewards do not enhance their own interests, but work in mutual solidarity within a united whole. This has of course fundamental implications for how mutual cooperation is developed. Conflicts are likely to reoccur if there is no trust between the parties, and as a result, there is more and more control and exercise of power in organizations.

Trust implies *faithfulness* as a distinguishing quality of stewardship. The leader is expected to begin in his or her own house. The stewardship and leadership is dependent upon behavior also in private matters, similarly as credible stewardship depends on carrying out responsibilities. This is about being trustworthy in living peacefully together. If there is a lack of concordance between faith and deeds, as sometimes is shown when there are internal conflicts and divisions, it will be difficult to act as peacemaker in society at large.[17]

In strong cross-cultural contexts, it is of course easy for identification with different cultures and religions to dominate over the common identity of a mutual responsibility within the wider identity of the church or the interreligious faith community. However, when the church in modern society is increasingly understood as an organization among others in civil society, and staff members

17. Brattgård, *God's Stewards*; Reumann, *Stewardship and the Economy of God*.

demand more of day-to-day coordination, the managerial responsibility of bishops may be stressed, while their prophetic voice for peace and justice is neglected.

In traditional cultures where religious identity is stronger there is, however, a far stronger respect for religious and traditional authority, to the extent that effective management may be too weak to coordinate activities. However, with the stewardship concept, the leadership role is servant oriented and a steward is equal among others in maintaining the identity and purpose of the organization. The leadership role is to induce awareness of the common identity and the long-term perspectives to maintain mutual responsibility, unity, and peace, while defining various responsibilities according to the gifts and talents among other staff, also seen as stewards of their particular resources. If the perception of the church is merely a sacred organization separate from secular society at large, then the prophetic role of the church in the world will be lost.

ECO-THEOLOGICAL STEWARDSHIP

The ecumenical bodies of Western churches had raised the ecological issues already in the 1970s. The World Council of Churches initiated the Justice, Peace, and Integrity of Creation program in 1976 and the Pope John Paul II declared "peace with God the creator and peace with all creation" in 1989. It is, however, only recently that ecological concerns have received wider serious attention as an alarming global problem, with reports on global warming and emission of carbon dioxide as being caused by the Western and industrialized world in particular. However, in a similar way as the justice issues, raised at a 1983 peace conference (Life and Peace, Uppsala) by the churches from the South, was dominated by the nuclear threats, seen by the North as the main focus, we may now suspect that issues of global justice might be overlooked in the race for global economic growth and ecological security for the West.

The new concepts of sustainable growth or sustainable development were criticized, however, from the side of the churches (Global Forum 1992) as it stressed the financial and technical aspects rather than issues of justice. David G. Hallman has instead used the concept of sustainable community in order to stress the mutual responsibility and inclusion of social and cultural aspects in addition to the natural. Sustainability is also not any unanimous ecological concept as it is focusing more on natural resources, while some theologians want to pay attention to the fact that humanity constitutes a part of the whole nature and cosmos.[18]

Also Meeks and other theologians with a global and ethical perspective have a similar inclusive interpretation and show how the problems of this narrow interpretation of stewardship have characterized the debate between modern (Western churches) and traditional (Eastern churches) churches. Orthodox churches wanted to keep together the two spheres of creation and salvation while Protestant churches of the West wanted to limit the stewardship idea to the natural and political spheres.

The Lutheran Church has, however, given important contributions to stewardship theology, and particularly Brattgård's study in the 1960s, *God's Steward*, was a pioneering work, even if he did not much touch on the natural issues of ecology, which became important much later. It is, however, a very rich and deep analysis of the Greek word *oikos* (house) with its many connotations. If we see Brattgård's study in the framework of ecological humanism and eco-theology it is, however, far deeper than the modern approaches to ecological philosophy.

The stewardship concept has at several occasions later been discussed as the stewardship of God's creation, but it has never really taken root when other Western and modern concepts of management and administration were introduced. In my view, this discussion developed as a compromise between Brattgård's interpretations of stewardship and the ecological awareness that emerged at the time.

---

18. McFague, *Models of God*; Grenholm and Kamergrauzis, *Sustainable Development*.

The Belief in Modern Rationality and the Economy of Grace

CONCLUSION

At the introduction of this chapter, I demonstrated how the Western culture and belief in modern rationality, growth, and national development is typically disembedded from the social context and the local cultural identity. As we noted in the introductory chapter also, Western religion and the church has had a significant role in the legitimizing of globalization, and therefore it will be interesting to go deeper in examining the role of modern religion in the process of globalization.

Modern management and economics seem to represent a closed rationality as issues of traditional culture, religion, morality and other non-measurable aspects are seen as irrational and therefore treated as externalities, which also will be further discussed in the following chapters.

The concept of stewardship I have explained above, based on the concept of a global household (*oikoumene*), thus serves as a model to link identity and structure of cultures and religions, as well as to integrate the sacred and profane aspects of human and material aspects of development. Institutional structures and economy are therefore ideally seen as a stewardship of identity.

It is therefore important to note that our understanding here of stewardship is not limited to the responsibility of a single caretaker that acts in a discretionary way to manage resources of the owner, which is a common misconception of the original meaning of the word. Stewardship is rather based on a common identity shared by all.

At the beginning of the twenty-first century, there is also a renewed awareness that spirit, humanity, and nature as a whole are correlated, as explained in the ecosophic worldview. Many institutions involved in the struggle for an increased awareness of ecological threats are also beginning to use the concept of stewardship rooted in the classical understandings of a household (*oikos*) where all are mutually dependent for their livelihood.

In the next chapter, I will take the point of departure from the Western churches and related foreign mission and development work in the traditional cultural context of East Africa. The issue of discussion is about the identity of a united church that is difficult to manifest due to the diversity of national, cultural, and ethnic identities involved, modern, as well as traditional. The main question is: *What could the roots of cultural conflicts and differences in the relations between receiving churches in the South and related churches in the West be? How can the stewardship concept contribute to ecumenical and interreligious unity as well as mutual sharing of resources?*

In chapter 3 I will further examine Western globalization with its pressures for modernization, progress, and growth in the society at large, and how this comes into conflict with a common moral identity related to social care, economic, and ecological justice. *What can the church and religion do to manifest a prophetic identity as a moral community in the world?*

In chapter 4 I will review some of the critique that has been raised against domination and expansion of the neo-liberal market economy. It shows that the stewardship philosophy stressing a mutual responsibility and accountability contrasts sharply with the free market view of competition and self-interest. A central question here is: *What is the role of modern religion in relation to modern economics? How can church and religion be stewards of their common identity of peace, unity, and justice regarding the critique of the globalization of modern economics and market domination?*

In chapter 5 I will further elaborate on the relations between state and church, which have been rooted in the Roman Empire since the Constantine age in the fourth century. With the help of the stewardship model of mutual responsibility among church members and local congregations, the prophetic identity of the church as a united body is highlighted. The important question then is: *What are the cultural or religious roots to the creation of power structures in society? What would a stewardship model and the ecosophic worldview mean for the transformation of power structures and what would manifest their identity as peace makers?*

Chapter 6 reviews some of the history of modern economics, showing how Western and Protestant ethics have provided legitimacy to the mainstream political economic systems. Even today, the market fundamentalism has become religiously inspired by the belief in "prosperity religion." An interesting question here is: *What*

The Belief in Modern Rationality and the Economy of Grace

can the identity of stewardship with an ecological philosophy do in order to promote social and social responsibility?

Chapter 7 makes problematic the impact of free market orientation on modern religion, which creates both a religious and secular rationalism and a separation of the sacred, human, and natural aspects, and thereby weakens the role of a prophetic church. The main question being asked is: *What can stewardship do in order to promote the identity of a united and prophetic church with a holistic view of mission?*

In chapter 8 I will review some of the main economic principles of some cultures and religions. *How is the philosophy of stewardship formulated in the diversity of cultures and religions? Is it possible to arrive at a common interreligious identity for peace and economic justice?*

In chapter 9 there is first a discussion on how the separation of faith and reason, or faith and deeds, are due to Western rationalizations and secularism. Some of the crucial questions are: *How can a stewardship of faith serve as an important precondition for the development of knowledge? What can the stewardship view do to help church and religion to live their identity and faith in actions and structure?*

Chapter 10 shows how various religions may seek deeper unity at the level of mystery, where there seems to be a much more common understanding of integrating the sacred and the profane aspects of religion. *What can the mystery of religions do to promote interreligious unity?*

In the final chapter, chapter 11, I make a concluding analysis with recommendations. With reference to the historical overview in the introductory chapter, I conclude that the institutional structures depended very much on the power of emperors and bishops, rather than being based on the original identity of a prophetic church of peace, unity, and justice. The still dominating hierarchical power structures appear to be related to patriarchal and political views of God above the state and the church. Therefore, the prophetic identity of the church seems to be out-rationalized. *What are the challenges of stewardship and the ecosophic worldview for the wider society? What can this model contribute to in the discussions about a common image of God in the world?*

2

The Loss of a Prophetic and Ecumenical Identity

FRAGMENTED IDENTITIES OF THE CHURCH

A MAJOR DIFFICULTY IN the manifestation of unity and peace is that there is a conflict between the identity of a united church and the different identities of various faith communities, cultures, and ethnicities that are being used to give legitimacy and power over resources. The understanding of church and related organizations for mission, social development, peace, cooperation, partnership, management, stakeholders, and so on are also typically dominated by the Western worldview of modernization and development.[1]

Even the word "mission" is often understood by some mission organizations, development agencies, and even churches as limited to the preaching of the gospel, and is used separately from social activities and diaconal work. Still, the etymology of the word suggests it is related to the overall purpose of the church (to fulfill its "mission"). In society in general, the religious "mission" is also understood as conversion and should be discouraged from a secular point of view. Consequently, the prophetic role of the church as a steward of God in the building of peace and justice is not well received.

1. Jonsson, *Narrow Management*.

PROBLEMS OF A FRAGMENTED CENTRALIZATION

At the beginning of the introduction, I referred to the study I made in some of the church organizations in East Africa receiving foreign aid for modern and social development. A major problem I saw as advisor and financial controller was that excessive fragmentation into development projects, bilaterally financed by Western donors for earmarked purposes, created a concentration of power to the central administration and to foreign aid organizations and governments. However, most of the local church work was funded through voluntary collections from congregational members. The planning, implementation, and evaluation of these projects was largely done according to Western models of management, which had been introduced with external support and management consultants from the US and Western Europe. The leaders of the church were also very much occupied in the management and administration, which could take most of their time.

The partner organizations and state aid agencies in the West most often considered it necessary to earmark aid for special purposes or projects and to demand specific progress reports, financial reports, audit reports, as well as evaluations for their particular project, in order to get access to support from their partner organizations and agencies. This fragmentation brought about a concentration of power in the hands of different institutional donors and the central administration channeling the aid; but it also brought power to regional administrations, which naturally also contributed to conflicts and problems of cooperation.

This created also a huge bureaucratic apparatus of control at every level, but this did not necessarily imply any improved transparency for local church members and congregations. On top of all this, it was increasingly difficult for those involved to get an overview of the integration of resources and priorities according to the needs and the overall identity of the church. This fragmentation and bilateral support contributed significantly to power concentration, which was legitimated by different cultural, ethnic, national, or religious identities.

The disregard for an ecumenical and united church body therefore resulted in an inferior utilization of existing surpluses on central and regional levels, and thus a locally integrated and united stewardship was difficult. This would have allowed a united church body to give priority within a comprehensive budget for the total needs as well as the total resources available. Further, it was recommended to exercise more long-term planning, with a focus on the overall identity of a united church, characterized by a mutual responsibility.

MARGINALIZATION OF LOCAL CONGREGATIONS

I have already argued that fragmentation into projects produced a centralization of power, which in turn led to disengagement of the local church congregations from the overall issues of a united and ecumenical identity with a mutual responsibility.

As a result of modern institutionalization, local community workers have increasingly become employed in higher-level administration; consequently, they have less time for direct voluntary work. In Western countries, an increasing number of people are instead employed in order to carry out activities that were earlier done on a voluntary basis. Organizational rationality in this regard has therefore reduced the power of local communities and voluntary workers. Democracy is still maintained in the formal elections, but voluntary engagement has been increasingly shifted to various committee meetings and executive boards. Centralization of power happens, as there is an increasing complexity of activities and operations, which requires the employment of experts, professional knowledge, and external funding.

One can discern similar developments in numerous voluntary religious and humanitarian organizations. It is not sufficient for public authorities to prioritize privatization and thereby strengthen civil society's organizational actors. Civil organizations as well as political bodies need to deepen their own democracy through countering the marginalization of their members' influences, which has occurred because of modern privatization as well as political centralization. This concerns especially those organizations that often lack support from their own members. Today there are a great many umbrella organizations, particularly in the South, where groups of employees, consultants and companies, as a result of privatization can procure large grants of aid simply by registering an organization, even if it is completely devoid of members. The church's identity as a body of many limbs or a community of believers has been pushed aside to the benefit of centrally coordinated structures that can manage large aid grants.

RESOURCE CONFLICTS

From the ecosophic view of the world, we would therefore need to pay much greater attention to interrelations between faith, politics, and economy. Different interests and power over resources tend, however, to fracture those forces striving to gain mutual cooperation and an understanding of an ecumenical and united church. Divisions and conflicts make it difficult for the ecumenical church community to maintain the idea of stewardship with mutual responsibility and accountability among all cooperating partners in the development. Our ecosophic model of stewardship means, for instance, that it is important to use all resources in a responsible way, which is difficult if external aid givers identify themselves only as donors but not as receivers as well. The financing of projects and the formulation of objectives is often short sighted, and the internal structures are commonly based on the strategies of the donating partners rather than internal strategies and preferences. This has come about, firstly, because of the insistence by modern culture of project rationality and fragmentation, which also has had an impact on various churches and religions. When the expectation is that churches should reflect unity and peace it is a special challenge for an ecumenical stewardship of resources.

Therefore to understand internal and complex conflicts, it is necessary to view them in relation to the external political and economic sources. This rationalization of external interests and goals, which also has an impact on the local united church, will be further explained in the following.

The Power of the West in the Economy of Grace

STEWARDSHIP FOR PEACE WITH UNITY AND JUSTICE

There is a great potential in the ecumenical understanding of stewardship when it comes to building of unity, peace, and justice within the church. We noted above how conflicts within the church are often linked to the globalization of institutional structures. The major conflict patterns confronting the globally changing world we see today often appear to involve fragmented centralization, or a modern version of a divide-and-rule strategy with terrorism, corruption, and competition for power of resources. Conventional approaches to peacemaking have been most often characterized by national and political competition over land territories and have not paid much attention to the economic injustice between rich and poor as one of the root causes of violence. This critique has been voiced at several ecumenical and interfaith conferences for the promotion of peace and justice,[2] particularly from the poor developing countries. In recent years, the urgent need for sustainable development and the combat against poverty have demonstrated that social conditions and the access to livelihood have become preconditions for an economy of peace. Parallel to the continuing threat from what has been termed "religious extremism," it is repeatedly argued that religion itself is not really the root cause, but can be misused in order to give legitimacy to power and even war.

However, the conventional tools for peace are mostly oriented towards managing conflicts identified from time to time between different parties. When it comes to root causes of conflicts it may, however, be necessary to look for new tools for peace or strategies involving culture, religion, power, or resources, which also highlights the prophetic role to manifest peace and justice.

Negotiation between conflicting nationalities, leaders, or parties is still the focus of debate in peace building, conflict management, conflict transformation, conflict resolution, or reconciliation. Many actors in what is now termed as the "civil society" are engaged in this work of managing conflicts, which receives considerable

2. LPI, "Papers and Presentations."

public support. And the conflicts have largely been seen in either an East-West or a North-South perspective.

Another dimension of global conflicts is the increasing differences between rich and poor that seems to come as a result of the globalization of modern economic growth theories. And today there is an escalating economic crisis as well as threats against the climate. In all of the approaches above the global strategy is either to manage conflicts between different parties, religions or ethnicities within nations or to fight against terrorism, which does not recognize that root causes for conflicts or terrorism may lie in the existence of growing social and economic injustice. There are global campaigns against poverty, but we do not see much campaigning against wealth and greed. It seems as if all people could become rich without threatening ecological concerns and future generations.

In my view, conflicts are not just between parties and there legitimate interests, but involve even evil forces sometimes far beyond the understanding of the actors themselves. There is an urgent need for restoration and reconciliation, which is necessary in order to deal with the demands for revenge and punishment. This is well explained in the *Art of Reconciliation*, which elaborates on the experiences from South Africa, and resembles similar principles outlined in the introduction.[3]

Modern conflict management theories appear, however, to be rooted in popular business management discourse, which even sees conflict as normal and a positive force to induce the desire for business growth and progress. Therefore, it should be necessary to go far deeper in the study of conflicts. "Structural violence" would be a more accurate description, if by peace we mean not just the absence of war, but also democracy, freedom, and economic justice. This is motivated as churches and religion in general can play an important role for peace and justice as the structures of power, ecumenical relations, or leadership may be signs of unity or conflict.

Violence related to the wider rationalized systems of laws, organizations, doctrines, regulations, economic systems, etc., of the churches or other religious bodies have, however, received almost

---

3. Villa-Vicencio, *The Art of Reconciliation*.

no attention in mainstream peace research. Peace studies from political macro perspectives reflect a kind of modern rationalization in that they often describe, categorize, and study the number of conflicts. To discover and understand institutional conflicts it will even be necessary to study the deeper processes of rationalization and the creation of organizations, which can induce conflicts or competition.

The Life and Peace Institute in Uppsala has done pioneering work in the development of tools for peace that go beyond the immediate settlement of conflicts at national and international levels. The approach goes commonly under the name of *Community Based Peace Building* where the role of women and traditional and religious leaders in the communities play a significant role in integrating the "life world" outside the institutional structures of society.[4]

To develop this approach further, the concept of stewardship as explained in the previous chapter should have great potential, which can challenge in particular religions and churches to contribute to peace within the ecumenical body as well as in the society at large.

PEACE IN THE BODY OF CHRIST

I would then like to stress that the idea of church stewardship is based on the theological identity that sees the church as a steward of God, and then related to the body of Christ for the manifestation of peace, love, and reconciliation. Conflicts are then not really "normal." Walter Vink talks about the same, for instance when he sees violence, power, culture, or spirit not as part of human identity, but rather as an autonomous force that has an impact on people. It often appears, for instance, that religious conflicts today are closely related to religion as *institutions,* like doctrines or power positions and organizations, rather than appearing in the local community of believers.

The popular understanding about the church in a secular society does, however, often limit the understanding of the church as

---

4. Pfaffenholz, *Community Based Peace Building.*

a traditional and sacred institution outside the profane sphere. The church is then seen very much as a non-government organization in civil society carrying out social development projects on behalf of the state. The sacred and religious sphere is then seen as a private concern. However, a united church also has a prophetical role as a sign for peace and justice, and should also raise her prophetic voice against secular political or market institutions whenever she feels their decisions and structures would threaten the needs of the children, the poor and oppressed who belong to the kingdom of God and are the identity of a prophetic church.

Therefore, it can be a particular challenge to the many different church institutions and faith communities to further develop mutual responsibility and accountability within the church in order to be a sign of ecumenical and interreligious unity. What I see as typical for the expansion of different organizations and projects is an "instrumental rationalization," where the overall purpose and identity of a common faith in peace may be "out-rationalized" by specific and formal doctrines. The continuous creation of organizations, laws, rules, structures, regulations, codes, or constitutions, may be contradictory to the overall purpose and the wider universal identity of the church. Therefore, they may turn into rather narrow and individual goals or confessions, which can receive financial support and national legitimacy.

CONCLUSION

In response to the initial questions set out in chapter 1, I conclude that much of the institutional structure of new churches in Africa have their roots in the various mission organizations, aid agencies, and voluntary aid agencies in the West, as well as the ethnic differentiations made by the national state. It was explained in new institutionalism theories as a "rationalization of a fragmented resource environment."[5]

This is done in relation to central administrations as well as different regional administrations, projects, congregations, and

---

5. Scott, *Institutional Environments*, 160.

departments. Most of the relations are even created bilaterally, which makes it difficult to exercise an integrated stewardship of resources within the church as a whole, seen as an integrated body of local congregations. Most of the aid is designated for different projects and priorities set by the donors or the central administration. This creates, according to the same theories, a fragmented centralization, and a highly structured and elaborated administration, with a lack of full transparency and accountability to local congregations, both in the receiving and donating churches.

The multiplicity of fragmented financial and progress reports for each project are sent to the donors. The Western state aid agencies and church-related organizations demand effective management and control from the recipients concerning their particular project, but they seem to lack the understanding that they themselves are part of mutual accountability, as indicated in the stewardship principle and the image of the body of Christ.

The challenge of stewardship would therefore be to develop an integrated and comprehensive planning that departs from the identity of a united and ecumenical church where the different traditional ethnicities and the various identities of different supporting partners are seen as resources and opportunities to strengthen a common identity and purpose. The role of stewardship seems now to be limited to the funding of the church, but not much according to the principles of mutual responsibility and accountability.

On top of that, the designation of external aid to local governments often within ethnically defined areas also contributes to intrastate conflicts. As a result there is a lack of trust and credibility regarding shared resources in the wider context, beyond ethnically or culturally defined areas.

The division between support from Western churches and foreign state aid agencies also contributes to the institutional differentiation between modern development projects receiving massive foreign aid and church-related work, which is much less supported. This often causes conflicts of identity between well-paid development workers and lowly paid voluntary workers from local congregations.

The Loss of a Prophetic and Ecumenical Identity

All these problems of disintegration should make it very important to highlight the challenges of the theology of stewardship and the prophetic identity of a united church as a body of Christ, as it was outlined in chapter 1. This should become particularly important in the education of pastors, evangelists, or missionaries as well as workers in what is called development.

Equally important would be to raise the question about the Western view of modern development contra the ecosophic worldview in formal education as well as in discussions in ecumenical conferences and courses. The mounting climate threats make it urgent to point out that stewardship is also a matter of a wider ecological philosophy stated in chapter 1. The West has in fact a huge ecological debt to the South and much of the resources given should therefore not be treated as a matter of dependence. Therefore, ecosophic stewardship involves learning about the interdependence of spirit, humanity, and nature as it was outlined in the preceding chapter.

3

Outrationalization of the Moral Impulse

IN THIS CHAPTER, we shall go deeper in analyzing the processes of rationalization, which is central to the understanding of Western culture and economic globalization with its belief in modern institutional rationality, growth, and progress, but often comes into conflict with demands for social, ecological, or economic justice.

The sociological philosopher Zygmunt Baumann has used the Weberian concept of rationalization to explain how the postmodern culture may involve an "out-rationalization of the moral impulse."[1] By refining it in terms of its contribution to the expanding economic culture so typical of ongoing modern globalization, and contrasting it with our model of stewardship from an ecosophic worldview, one can obtain a wider and deeper understanding of the meaning of mutual responsibility. Most of the empirical support I am referring to is taken from my research in business administration.[2]

The process of rationalization comprises various types of rationality in order to justify power, but I will limit myself to the "instrumental rationality," which involves typical emphasis on the

---

1. Baumann, *Postmodern Ethics*.

2. See Jonsson, *Narrow Management* and *Att vara eller inte vara kyrka*; Stieglitz, *Wither Socialism?*; Duchrow, *Faith Communities*; Fehr, "Economic Man"; Korten, *When Corporations Rule the World* and *Alternatives to Economic Globalization*.

methods or means rather than on any overall social or moral purpose. This occurs, for instance, with investing money without accurately comprehending moral implications or social responsibilities. And it happens when profit-orientation blindly directs resources to certain profitable areas while others lack resources, even though this may have immense repercussions for support to the whole. It also takes place when banks lend money to those who already have funds, because it facilitates repayment. The rationalization process explains how modern economics, capitalism, religious secterism, or nationalism as ideological systems, tends to be more important than inter-human relations or ecological and social concerns.

However, from the ecosophic stewardship perspective applied, we have to also realize the means themselves are not just rational, but injected with values and culture. The means would then be seen as assets or values, which are to be developed in order to promote a common and overall social purpose. The goal or the belief is not in economic growth or even modern development.

DOWNSIZING OF SOCIAL CARE

It is well-known, for instance in Sweden and Europe, that public organizations involved in social healthcare or schools face difficulties in meeting the demands for social care due to an increasing demand for downsizing of costs and taxes as well as the demand to increase economic growth.

In such situations, the leadership will face conflict between the demand to implement the overall identity effectively on one hand, and the financial constraints and detailed regulations that they are subject to from politicians, economists, and public authorities. This is evident, for instance, in many television documentaries on the privatization of social care and schools. A very common image that appears in many of these observations is that some political parties insist on reduced taxes, but on the other hand they indirectly tolerate a violation of the overall health policy. Professional education stresses loyalty toward patients or students, to whom they will impart the best of their knowledge and experience concerning healthcare and education. What happens then is that healthcare centers may run into huge deficits and the number of students in each class is doubled. In general, politicians seem to lack such professional knowledge and experience and therefore depend wholly on financial and other measurable methods of control.

Viewed from the stewardship perspective outlined above there seems to be a lack of both mutual responsibility and accountability between politicians and professionals. The politicians govern through fragmented and financial control of expenditures rather than overall long-term goals and regulations. Professional staff in schools and health centers, as stewards, may therefore become powerless and frustrated through this kind of fragmented centralization.

The new and popular model of market orientation in the provision of public service also makes it difficult to exercise a mutually responsible stewardship of given resources. The overall professional guidelines and social quality may be easily set aside when private entrepreneurs compete with the lowest possible price. The social service becomes a mere business commodity to be bought and sold in a market.

THE BELIEF IN ACTION AND PROGRESS

The pressure for economic growth and rapid development compels those who are otherwise responsible to abandon long-term objectives, or to disregard ethical demands for peace, democracy, and justice. The pressure can come from shareholders—lenders or individuals who wish to see a rise in share prices. This affects many leaders today, who sometimes have a pronounced activity-orientation progress. It is viewed as imperative to illustrate energy and efficiency but may be less urgent to allow overarching questions concerning identity and purpose. This forces the presentation of concrete and measurable results prematurely to what is actually both possible and sustainable in the long run.

The preoccupation with short-term results simultaneously exposes a lack of trust in the management or enterprise, which

Outrationalization of the Moral Impulse

necessitates closer mutual relations and community at a more fundamental social and ethical level. The stewardship approach, however, should take seriously the sustainable use of its own talents, time, spirit, and vision, rather than belief in what external and large-scale funding will bring.

THE BELIEF IN HIGH TECHNOLOGY

The most recent global development of informational technology (IT) is typical of a technical rationalization, which is intimately connected with Western modernization. Large sums of money are invested as the latest and most advanced technology has to be installed because it is modern, without real evaluation given to what will best promote a sustainable use of resources in the long run or to give priority to other social needs.

The pressure for modern technical rationalization on a global scale will need a lot of exploration of natural resources and minerals, which have created competition for power and even conflicts and violence in some areas, particularly in Africa, Central Asia, and the Middle East. The ecosophic view on stewardship does not treat the local resources as means for modern economic growth from a Western anthropocentric perspective. Rather, institutions are created based on a mutual understanding of interdependence, equality, and justice between nations and people. There is also understanding that natural resources may be limited, should be used for the future generations as well, and should not bring harm to other people.

THE PRESSURE FOR MEASURABILITY

Modern and fragmented rationality conflicts with the wider idea of ecumenical stewardship, especially when measurability becomes indispensable and obligatory for evaluating activities or enterprises and for the procurement of external funding to modern development projects. The application of measurability to social or spiritual purposes and goals, which are hard to quantify, makes it difficult to take account of local human resources and qualities, as these cannot easily be substantiated. External aid is typically technical and monetary and sometimes easy to get, particularly if it is tied to the export of goods from the donor country. The stewardship approach departs from an initial exploration of local resources, be they material or spiritual.

A predilection for measurability is also revealed when faith communities are obliged to report their accomplishments in terms of economic statistics, project reports, membership statistics, etc., and when these all provide a rational and factual basis for decision-making and evaluation or for recording and controlling activities. Compared to our stewardship model it is problematic when the presentation of quantified data and documentation is separated from the actual work, and therefore it tends to be used to control from the top and externally in a way that is not so transparent. Simply speaking, one does not see what the figures represent. As a contrast with our stewardship model of mutual accountability, we can see that an emphasis is placed on the role of power and control, with little consideration of the overall mission and the fact that this mandate has been given in mutual trust and faith.

INSTITUTIONAL RATIONALITY

Institutional rationality leads easily to a *disengagement* of people who may not produce enough result as success cannot be obtained unless there are precise boundaries, within which progress is measured and controlled. The demand for measurability creates fences around institutions and projects through the formation of distinct boundaries in order to measure membership in countries, organizations, departments, projects, and other entities. This enables actors to measure growth and progress within the framework of their own entity and legitimate their own progress. However, this renders more difficult a mutual cooperation. It also leads to the neglect of an awareness of a common, wider identity and background, which the concept of stewardship, with its essence of mutual responsibility and accountability, takes into particular consideration. Growth and success is obvious in an external sense, but rationalism and competition for power that follows in its wake creates fragmentation and marginalization of, for instance, foreigners, who may not easily fit in.[3]

The result-orientation and pressure for growth requisites of measurability and result evaluation (for instance GNP) leads to the exclusion of various social values with irrational elements, which are not considered to enhance the growth. If the frontiers between the European Union (EU) and other countries were wholly open, for instance, it would be impossible for the Union to control its own economic growth. It becomes necessary to develop an effective bureaucracy, even if it does not promote peace and justice. The rationalization process has a close connection to self-interest, and is linked to significant actors who seek to measure their own achievement.

The EU, for instance, is an organization that, according to its constitution, simply demands effective growth and expansion, above all in narrow economic respects. The market-oriented culture in effect makes the EU an enterprise in contradistinction to people, who strive after a mutual sustainability with a shared responsibility. Among other things, this makes it especially difficult to incorporate as new members those countries that cannot demonstrate sufficient economic strength. Likewise, the EU cannot easily take action over environmental and solidarity matters if the economic interests of member states are jeopardized. The original idea of the EU as a peace project has now rather turned into an economic project. The pressure for rationalization and economic growth in poor countries like Greece has meant that they must first cut down on public expenditures like social security and pensions before they can get further support from richer EU members, as our ecosophic model of stewardship would call for.

---

3. Scott, *Institutional Environments*; Jonsson, *Narrow Management*.

The Power of the West in the Economy of Grace

NATIONALIZATION AS A MODERN PROJECT

Nationalization was of tremendous importance for the emerging nations of the Third World, not least in the period after the Second World War. It is reasonable to claim that these nations were compelled to accept the Western criteria of nationality in order to become part of the world community and to gain legitimacy and assistance for modern economic development. Issues such as self-determination, independence, and self-support that developed in this context were to a large extent characterized by a type of modern rationalization, which did not much recognize the local cultural or ethnic boundaries. It is at least partly in this perspective that we need to understand how power and domination developed from the aid givers in the West.

Nationalism was the main motive behind the extermination of Jews as they were seen by the Nazis as a foreign element in the growth and progress of a "pure" German nation. Zygmunt Baumann, the great postmodern ethicist, thinks the Holocaust was not solely based on anti-semitism.[4] The extermination of Jews could be implemented at a massive scale because it was systematically organized in a detailed and rationalistic manner. The Jews were therefore concentrated into specific locations. The Holocaust should therefore be a reminder of an unrestrained rationalism that we occasionally observe in today's economic and political culture. We can for instance notice how immigrants, the elderly, or the marginalized may be assumed to impede economic growth and rationality.

ECONOMIC INJUSTICE

A major problem is that processes of modern economic rationalization imply huge and increasing gaps between rich and poor. More people become much richer, but even more become poorer. The stewardship model of institutional structure and economy applied is on the other hand an inclusive model stressing a mutual

---

4. Baumann, *Postmodern Ethics*, 119–29.

interdependence between people and resources as well as between generations.

The impact of a rationalization process implies a continuous division into new and more distinct entities that operate as result units where power over their resources can be controlled within a particular project, but not shared with others. This extensive fragmentation makes it more and more difficult to exercise mutual responsibility and a wider and integrated stewardship of resources.

The contemporary emphasis on formulating specific objectives necessitates that these are expressed in measurable terms such as budget figures, hours, quantities, or in the form of geographic areas, all with the purpose of ensuring efficiency and results. In order to enlarge the share of the market and to be able to measure this, it becomes necessary to identify a narrow target group for one's products and selections so as to maximize own earnings and maximum return on invested capital.

This may first seem self-evident and unproblematic, but from our integrated stewardship perspective it is highly problematic because the demand for greater efficiency and growth based on certain interests can easily bring about more administrative control from the top. Another problem is that the identities and categories created (for example consumers, employees, pensioners, or electors) convey various self-understandings to each person, which can shatter inclusive identity and self-understanding within a wider context. The globalization of the economy can result in a kind of market democracy where influence derives solely through self-interested and rational choice in the market, with no access to information about how the money is accumulated in the hands of others. This tendency combined with political institutionalism reduces the individual's opportunities to take mutual responsibility in society. I am then not referring to the creation of institutions that are locally rooted, but to those controlled at a macro-economic level and which chiefly function as the rules of the game for principal actors in the so-called "free" market.

The same type of institutionalization is expressed when international bodies such as the United Nations focus on specific themes for limited periods. In these instances, certain target groups receive attention and an end date is set when a particular objective shall be completed with the information of the numbers assisted. This, for example, is the case when the United Nations Development Program (UNDP) will reduce the numbers living in poverty by 50 percent before the year 2015. This should not be viewed with skepticism as the effort is praiseworthy, but such rationalizations in the form of measurable objectives can lead to the misconstruction of the overall aspiration of solidarity. Since one of the implementation strategies of this policy is the strengthening of the market driven economy, an attack on poverty cannot make use of redistribution between rich and poor. Arising from the overall aim of mutual solidarity one could rather have made an attack on wealth, since there are hardly enough resources and possibilities to make all rich. In this case, the poor are reduced to an economic and institutional category of poverty.

Rationalization and institutionalization, with exact targets and figures etc, contributes furthermore to the perception that poverty is easier to endure if there are only half as many who are poor, even when this group should plausibly be much poorer than today. In addition, if the aim is rapid economic growth through campaigns, it is likely that those who are least poor will be the first who receive help. The argument is that in this case result-orientation represents a part of global economic growth, in which transnational corporations control the world. Consequently, it might seem as if the power of the rich would correspond with the interests of the poor, which in all likelihood will increase the risk for conflict and imply greater economic injustice.

Such measurability may turn into a problem for public authorities and organizations when visible results become more important than the remedy of real problems and local needs. Difficulties can arise if short-term efficiency in healthcare programs, for instance, leads to the marginalization of poor and sick, which may demand a lot of personal care and money without immediate results.

CONCLUSION

The impact of modern globalization with its pressures for rationalization, economic growth, and progress cause, in particular, conflicts in relation to traditional, social, and cultural identities. The belief in rationality and project aid make it difficult to give priority to the overall purpose of peace, justice, and sustainable development, and then develop the local sources needed to support it.

It is also necessary to question the universal spread of modern political and business economic education and literature, where rational self-interest and market orientation dominates. Instead, schools and universities need to introduce literature, which also includes traditional institutions of stewardship that pays a greater attention to a diversity of local, spiritual, and cultural resources. The strategy of stewardship also helps highlight the ecological philosophies of interdependence as an alternative to modern management, where neoclassical and modern economics now dominate also outside the Western world. In the next chapter, I shall review some of the critique raised against these theories.

4

The Critique against Globalization of Modern Economics

IN THIS CHAPTER, I will review some of the theoretical critique, which has been raised against modern economics and business concerning their focus on continuous economic growth and free market competition. This appears to lead to a disengagement of social responsibility as well as identification with the local cultures and religions outside the global business community.

An increasing part of research in economics demonstrates that the strong belief in a modern economic rationality, which is generally based on individual self-interest and financial rewards to motivate progress, does not get real scientific support. Still many economists in the established profession have for long believed in the "homo-economicus" and a self-regulating market. Professor Ernst Fehr and others have, however, made several cross-cultural studies in what is called "neuro-economics" and found that human beings are far more altruistic and socially cooperative than what is assumed by most mainstream economists.[1]

Peter Soderbaum has perhaps provided the most thorough and radical critique against neoclassical economics, which he regards as too narrow and does not recognize the social, ecological,

---

1. Fehr, "Economic Man."

and ethical aspects nor the possibility of other alternatives.[2] His personal view, institutional economics, is not offered as the single best way for everyone but the author understands it as a better possibility to deal with problems of sustainable development than mainstream economics. Above all, Soderbaum asks for a pluralistic dialogue and an integration of all members of society.

As a result of globalization, modern economics of the free market is now increasingly encountering traditional cultures and religions all over the world, where they have to pay greater attention to social responsibility as the globalization of institutional structures are largely disintegrated from the social and cultural context.

ECONOMIC GLOBALIZATION AND FRAGMENTATION

In my previous study about international church aid referred to above, *Narrow Management*, it was shown that modern economic globalization is characterized by an ongoing process of rationalization,[3] which in turn created a typical differentiation between the sacred and the secular and thus also between religion and modern economics.

Modern economics often assumes that self-interest is a natural law and implies an ongoing process of rationalization, which leads to a dichotomy between ethics, culture, religion, and economy. However, modern economics such as neoclassical economics have come under increasing critique, also from ecumenical perspectives, particularly since the emergence of globalization in the beginnings of 1980s.[4] Mainstream economists[5] usually refer back to Adam Smith and the "invisible hand of God," when they argue that economic growth automatically will imply social benefits for others. Friedman says for instance, "ethics means to apply the will of the

2. Soderbaum, *Understanding Sustainability*.
3. Scott, *Institutional Environments*; Jonsson, *Narrow Management*.
4. See Meyer, *Institutional Structure*; Stieglitz, *Wither Socialism?*; Nelson, *Economics as Religion*.
5. Friedman, "The Social Responsibility."

owners of business." Modern economic rationality and the Western model of welfare are then taken for granted as the overall goal that will eventually bring welfare for all. Thus, the discussion on ethics is used to legitimate the power of capitalism, and the only choice to be made is therefore between different types of modern economics, such as the liberal market economy and the communist model of planned economy. Since the collapse of the Soviet Union, the Western model of market economics has dominated the economic globalization and seeks also legitimacy from the Western church, which I shall come back to later.

In the new age of globalization with Western transnational corporations penetrating other traditional cultures, beyond the reach of national political regulations we can on the other hand see an increased awareness and critique from social, religious, and environmental activists under the banner of Corporate Social Responsibility (CSR).[6] This development has also been supported by the employees and labor unions that do not wish to be connected with companies that do not respect human rights and the respect for environmental concerns.

The conclusion of the new trends of globalization and the "remaking of world order" can even be seen as a "clash of civilizations" as argued by Huntington.[7] On one side, we have economic self-interest and power of modern cultures giving legitimacy to the power of the West, and on the other side we have traditional cultures and religions giving legitimacy to traditional power structures in the East and South. That demonstrates further the importance of promoting mutual interest and responsibility. And it should be no secret that prevailing rationalities of modern economic power structures contribute a lot to fragmentation, conflicts, and mistrust from traditional cultural and religious identities.

The critique of the modern economic system emphasize in general that it marginalizes the needs of the local community, the rural development and access to livelihood, as well the traditional culture and the ecological economics. New models are also

6. Korten, *When Corporations Rule the World*; Carroll, *Business and Society*.

7. Huntington, *The Clash of Civilizations*.

The Critique against Globalization of Modern Economics

suggested in order to pay attention to ethical concerns. However, so far little has been done to develop models in light of the multicultural and multireligious contexts of local and global economies today in order to promote mutual responsibility.

ECUMENICAL CRITIQUE

Demands for a new economic order have come in particularly from interreligious and ecumenical bodies that have recommended new aid policies promoting economic justice and campaigns to eradicate poverty. On an international level, the World Council of Churches has heavily criticized the World Bank for its theories of structural adjustment, which implied a downsizing of social welfare support and the shift to cash crops in order to pay for imports and repayment of their debts to Western banks.

In a report from World Alliance of Reformed Churches[8] that has taken account of the views among different faith communities and social movements facing globalization, it is stated that the domination of financial capital and technology marginalizes social responsibility and leads to human rights violations. From a theoretical perspective, the neoclassical economy is criticized for its assumption that self-interest is the best motor for development and economic growth determines possible allocations for social needs. The consequence of this statement would, of course, be that there is not much space for reallocation of resources to overall social needs and the poor.

It is also interesting to note that Muslim communities, as well as all other religions contributing to the study, stressed that peace and global justice is in fact a spiritual matter of concern. The Choran proclaims, for instance, "Do justice; it is closest to piety." It also says the poor and weak (*mustadàfin*) are the ones who become the "leaders and shall inherit the earth."

My conclusion of all the statements in this report is that the basic underlying value of solidarity with the poor is largely similar in all the faith communities. On top of that, it is very congruent

---

8. Duchrow, *Faith Communities and Social Movements*.

with the UN declarations of human rights, stating that all human beings should act with mutual solidarity and brotherhood.

However, in my view it seems that the main problem also for the faith communities is how to live and develop institutional structures that reflect the overall and common identity of peace and unity. The need to do this is also what is often emphasized in writings about stewardship.[9] Hall says that since the introduction of state religion of Christendom by Constantine the essence of stewardship has not had any real meaning, but that this system is now being disestablished. If we look particularly at the Christian faith traditions today we can find less critique against economic globalization in some of the faith communities with a more conservative outlook in society. Van den Berg has, for instance, made a thorough exploration of official policy documents among different Christian faith traditions and found that Catholic as well as modern evangelicals do not question the present market system of the West, although they seem to prefer a cooperative mode of production.[10] It is rather the mainline, Protestant churches, feminist economists, and liberal theologians who criticize the neoclassical economics and emphasize that the free market system does not pay enough attention to common interests as environment protection, human rights, and social responsibility.

NEW DEVELOPMENT POLICIES

Previous development policies have often been criticized for their neoclassical economic thoughts, which underlined the need for financial and technical investments in large-scale projects and required heavy external support in money and foreign personnel. The number of projects expanded enormously as new donors entered the scene and new goals and needs were identified in the image of the Marshall plan after the Second World War. The rapid increase of dollars from oil revenues in 1970s deposited in Western banks led to a huge increase of loans to the developing countries in order to

9. Hall, *The Steward*.
10. van den Berg, *God and the Economy*.

The Critique against Globalization of Modern Economics

get good return on their investments. The visions of development failed however and resulted often in inefficiency, corruption, and top-down planning and debt crisis.

In new policies on social development and aid to poor countries, international social scientists and public policy makers have, however, underlined the need for mutual accountability and local empowerment. A group of researchers within the EU framework have come to the conclusion that the aid needs to be coordinated and that the receiving countries need to take ownership of their own development in order to make aid effective,[11] which is commensurate with or model of stewardship.

What, in my opinion, is still missing is a critical analysis of the underlying economic cultures and the Western-oriented management models and market orientation, which in great part still departs from the rather narrow neoclassical economic paradigm. The assumption in that is economic science is objective and value free, and therefore it will best contribute to economic welfare and justice. The belief in modern economics is still dominating as the globalized market system is based on the belief in competition between self-interested business actors. However, modern market economy through competition is typically short-term and fragmented and is, in my view, neither congruent with the visions in the Paris Declaration nor the stewardship model with mutual responsibility outlined in chapter 1.

Another new trend is the institution of micro loans instead of conventional aid from the West. This "new" idea has received large support from the research by Mohammed Yunus and Grameen Banks, who received the Nobel's Peace Prize in 2006. This research has concluded that poverty is best eliminated through small-scale loans to local households organized by poor women (microcredit). This form of support is expanding rapidly and has led to new economic thinking based on traditional cultures with greater social cohesion, although still supported by modern technologies. However, it is probably not the technique itself but rather the underlying culture of local and mutual responsibility and the

---

11. OECD, *The Paris Declaration*.

involvement of women, which in my view have contributed to the success. The micro loans have however encountered serious problems when banks charge excessive fees and interest to cover for risk and administration, which poor borrowers cannot pay in the long run, therefore running out of business. This in fact is a violation of the stewardship principles of integration.

The business principles of the modern market economy are largely adopted from the West and are therefore not really suited to local and traditional cultural identities. In a study published by the Swedish International Development Agency (Sida) the foreign governments are challenged to change even the modern development strategies for the benefit of the poor rural areas in the South where the food production takes place.[12]

This concern is also reflected in the concept of sustainable society, rather than sustainable development, which could be more inclusive of social, religious, and cultural identities in addition to the economic and natural environment. The modern concept of sustainable development has also been criticized by ethicists and theologians for its focus on the scarcity of resources in the industrialized world, without really considering the need for a more fair distribution of resources between the rich and the poor and for the benefit of future generations as well.[13]

GLOBAL ETHICS

In the discussion about global ethics, there is sometimes a belief in universal ethics or common values, which are also needed in economics. However, it seems that demands for universalism could lead to a standardization of rules and norms, which also may out-rationalize the moral impulse. I follow Grenholm and Kamengrauzis when they say that modern global ethical rules or human rights declarations for sustainable development may not allow for a just redistribution of resources according to the needs in each particular situation, and which may be suffering the most from

12. Havnevik, Negash, and Beyene, *Of Global Concern*.
13. Grenholm and Kamergrauzis, *Sustainable Development*.

environmental degradation and climate changes.[14] There is thus a risk that a universal system of ethical codes will be dominated by the modern and Western economic culture of globalization at the expense of minorities and traditional cultures. This modern culture is typical of an instrumental rationalization that will guide the formulation of rules and regulations and which can out-rationalize the moral impulse and traditional cultural identities being difficult to measure and formulate in legal and financial terms for each particular context.[15]

What I mean also is that it is not just a question of universal ethical codes and norms or new financial systems, but that ethics needs to be integrated within the institutional structure itself. The idea of mutual responsibility inherent in the stewardship theory promotes the kind of ethics and responsibility that is needed. The conventional, modern, and technical understanding of economics is therefore too narrow and needs to be subjected to critical analysis as part of the quest for an ecosophic economy, which will be discussed later. The out-rationalization of the moral impulse suggested by Baumann has probably eliminated overall social purposes in business, and the moral sentiment of the so-called "invisible hand of God," that was previously assumed by Adam Smith.[16]

FEMINIST ECONOMICS

Many feminist scholars, such as Julie Nelson and many others, have contributed to feminist economics, which takes seriously the basic meaning of economy as a household. By the 1990s, it had become recognized as an established field within economics. Feminist economics call attention to the importance of non-market activities, such as childcare and domestic work, to economic development. This stands in sharp contrast to neoclassical economics where those forms of labor are unaccounted for as non-economic phenomena.

14. Ibid.
15. Baumann, *Postmodern Ethics*; Jonsson, *Narrow Management*.
16. Wilson, *Economics, Ethics and Religion*.

Including such labor in economic accounts removes substantial gender bias because women disproportionately perform those tasks.

It should also be quite clear that feminist economists are generally critical of the mainstream understanding of Western globalization, which they see as gender-biased. From a global perspective, experiences of men and women, even within the same household, may often be so different that examining economics without gender can be misleading. Mainstream economists often see globalization as an ongoing integration of the world into one, economic space through the flow of goods, capital, and money; and thereby they exclude some women and the disadvantaged. The uniformity of globalization experiences across all populations therefore depicts the political and Western view of globalization inappropriately. Feminist economists, and even those who criticize mainstream economics from ethical perspectives, explain that the concept of globalization itself is gender-biased, because its depiction as value free, dominant, unified, and intentional is inherently masculinized and undemocratic.[17]

My own experience from Africa is also that men generally control the earnings from cash crops while women are still expected to provide food and clothing for the household, their traditional role in the African family, along with labor to produce cash crops. Thus, women suffer significantly from the transition away from subsistence food production towards specialization and trade. Similarly, since women often lack economic power as business owners, they are more likely to be hired as cheap labor, and often involved in exploitative situations.

CONCLUSION

The main critique that has been raised against modern economics, growth, and progress is that social, ethical, spiritual and ecological concerns are being ignored both in decision making of business, and economic theory. The critique also concerns mainstream

---

17. Nelson, *Economics for Humans*; Sen, *On Ethics and Economics*; Bergeron, "Political Economy Discourses."

The Critique against Globalization of Modern Economics

economists who usually maintain they are objective, neutral, and are just following a natural law, or the invisible hand of God (e.g., Adam Smith). Ecological economics has raised a lot of critique against neo-classic economics and means that such theories are neither social, economic, nor ecologically sustainable. Feminist economists usually agree to this but also add that modern institutional and economic systems are typically male dominated and do not include the value of the homework carried out by women in the local household.

The critique has usually ended in suggestions for transfigurations into new economic systems or management models. The ecosophic worldview departs however from the view that there is a close interrelation between the divisions of spirit, humanity and nature, and there should also be a need to question the Western and egocentric worldview assumed in modern economic literature.

My conclusion concerning the critique is also that the same institutional structures, theories, and processes are being adopted almost all over the world as a result of Western globalization, without realizing that they carry with them values and cultures, which are not socially or culturally embedded.[18] Thus, there is a particular challenge to introduce alternative models as suggested above and ecosophic philosophies in schools.

With the application of stewardship theory in business corporations, the purpose should rather be formulated as "production of goods and services are for the welfare of all" rather than profit-oriented management. Profit could be seen as positive result and, of course, a condition for long-term financial sustainability, but not as an overall purpose as it is usually stated in the constitution of business companies. This should also far better create public support and legitimacy for the business world as a whole.

The model of stewardship and the ecosophic worldview implies also that all resources should be responsibly used in order to effectively and justly contribute to the welfare of all. Many social development actors maintain also that mutual interest, responsibility, and cooperation is the only valid principle for long-term

---

18. Giddens, *The Consequences of Modernity*.

sustainability. This model of stewardship is therefore a concept that could have support in the multi-cultural contexts, which is typical of the global society today.[19] I will further elaborate on this in the following chapters.

---

19. Meeks, *God the Economist*; Hall, *The Steward*.

5

Institutionalization of Religion

THE DISCUSSION HERE IS a deeper analysis on the impact of Western globalization in relation to the identity of a united church. The New Testament image of the kingdom of God seems to have been institutionalized into a diversity of denominations, churches, confessions, and sects, which induce conflicts and disintegration in relation to the overall identity of the church. The belief in rationality and growth seems therefore to be something that has diluted the identity of a united church.

DIFFERENTIATION BETWEEN SPIRITUAL AND MATERIAL MATTERS

Weber argued that modern and economic rationality suppressed traditions, culture, and religion.[1] One of the principal characteristics of modern culture is the desire to act rationally based on self-interest, which of course will also have an impact on religious organizations. To successfully win an argument today, one should accordingly employ such notions as rationality and the free market competition in order to fit into modern culture. Traditional culture instead relies on religion, ethnicity, and tradition for the justification of authority. Sociologist of religion Mark Chaves states that

1. Weber, *Economy and Society*.

religious authority is being diminished in Protestant denominations in relation to administrative and economic authority, and he interpreted this as "internal secularization."[2]

Internal secularization in my usage of the term, does not, however, only explain a declining religious authority, but more typically a differentiation between spiritual and material matters that differ from the identity of a united church as a sign of peace and justice in the world. Religion may or may not increase in membership and institutions, but it is typically privatized, which eliminates its prophetic identity in the world at large. Therefore, internal secularization can be seen as the direct result of the market-oriented culture of Western and modern globalization, now turning into a market society including religious services as well.

Following the same logic, it would not be very strange to assume that vertical structures would instead reflect an image of God who is at the top of the institutional structure itself, although invisible. This is in contrast to the stewardship view presented, where mutual responsibility and accountability in itself would fulfill the accountability to God. On the other hand, I consider that power in postmodern society has received new dimensions, in part through the institutionalization of a multiplicity of religious beliefs in modern society, and partly because faith has become privatized and is now mainly a question of a variety of understandings human beings can adopt. God and God's kingdom may then be comprehended or assumed to be separate from the world rather than manifested through the spirit, humanity, and nature.

Modern sociologists of religion usually have a transcendent understanding of religion. However, they have not really departed from an identity of religion that integrates sacred as well as profane matters. Seeing the church as a community, household, or family part of the world makes then of course a difference. Church historians have seen the church more as an institution, and studies about the church have been a practical sub-discipline to theology and largely included mapping the growth and development of various ecclesiastical organizations and denominations, as well as clergy's performance with services, liturgy, etc. However, the development

---

2. Chaves, "Intraorganizational Power."

of leadership and organizational structures of the church have not been informed or guided by the wider identity of the church as a body of Christ acting in mutual responsibility and accountability between various members and units in the organization and the world at large. Such understandings are, however, commonly developed by ecumenical and feminist theologians.[3]

Conventional and secular forms of organization, aid, or practices for conflict management can therefore come into conflict with the stewardship concept and Christian ethics because modern rationalism and reason brought about further tension between faith and deeds, the religious and the secular. This unity, however, is most central to the understanding of the prophetic identity of the church in the world.

STATE AND CHURCH AS TWO KINGDOMS OF GOD

The institutional division between state and church in Protestant churches in the sixteenth century implied in my view a rationalization of the Kingdom of God into two spheres of government. It was a division between the role of the State to care for the creation and the role of the church to preach the gospel and care for the souls of the people. This also implied a kind of fragmented centralization, with a typical rationalization of the prophetic identity of the church, seen as something separate from this world. Today the secular State has entirely different associations than the world of peace, unity, and love that Jesus sought to explain.

The common modern perception has been that stewardship is primarily concerned with the earth; organization, social work, ecological concerns, and the economy are, foremost, part of creation and the mundane rather than part of salvation, which is associated with the reconciliation of human beings with God. According to our stewardship model, we would also treat the gospel as a gift of grace. Moreover, the stewardship perspective embraces both the receiving and giving of God's grace and love for all people. This understanding of stewardship and the church universal seen as a

---

3. McFague, *Models of God*; Bosch, *Transforming Mission*; Mudge, *The Church as a Moral Community*.

united body makes it easier to keep together the two realms of sacred and profane activities. Conversely, the church should present itself, also in social and political concerns, as a trustworthy sign of peace and solidarity to the world and society.

It is now usually accepted in modern societies that the state is separate from the church, but it is increasingly demanded from the political authorities that religion is a private matter and should even be separate from public society as a whole. Consequently, worldly issues such as power structures and economy, as well as political concerns of the society, would not really be the concern for the church. Therefore, the structures of the church have been influenced by thoughts and values other than those derived from the theological identity of the church as a body of Christ.

The rationalization into two kingdoms legitimizes, as I see it, the interrelation of the power of the state and the power of the church, which is not in accord with the concept of a prophetic church identity. The differentiation should have come about during the early reformation period as the church's leadership in a way agreed to divide the power in order for the church to avoid too much involvement from the state in internal church matters. This gave, however, legitimacy to the removal of social and political issues from the church.

In my view, the stewardship concept has thus been marginalized as a result of the internal secularization of the church. Viewed from an ecosophic worldview as well as the ecumenical identity outlined in the first chapter, the understanding of stewardship of grace makes it important to see that the sacredness is part of the world through the identification with the poor and oppressed.

RELIGIOUS FUNDAMENTALISM

The rationalization of faith is sometimes expressed as fundamentalism, but is distinctively different from a stewardship of grace where faith is seen as a matter of *trust* rather than as a matter of *belief*. Fundamentalism happens when, for instance, the power of the clergy or church leaders may demand a strict observance of such institutions as regulations, laws, and the doctrines of faith, which imply a kind of out-rationalization of prophetic gifts from the economy of grace. These gifts are created to safeguard and even reform the church's doctrine, but the religious rationalism disengages the laws from the gospel, which instead should form the basis of the prophetic church, its meaning, or its ultimate purpose. A similar legalism, by the way, can affect other areas such as political ideology and modern economics. Fundamentalism is therefore not just a religious phenomenon.

Religious doctrine and symbols can have their own intrinsic merit but remain disengaged from the world that they symbolize or represent. Therefore, the church may not always understand why the involvement in the promotion of peace and justice is part of its mission.

The requirement to abide strictly by these regulations can even result in the curtailment of care for individual people and become a dilemma for the church that aspires to maintain the profound substance of faith as a matter of grace, if it is viewed from the stewardship perspective we have explained.

PIETISTIC RATIONALISM

Religious rationalism is found frequently in modern revival movements, expressed as a narrow stress on a privatized or an individualized faith. If the understanding of conversion is mainly restricted to an inner experience of religiosity, without being directly connected to the social context and within a united church, one could speak about "pietistic rationalism." Pietism implies a methodical and controlled, ascetic way of personal life, which suggests a modern, devout, reformed, or rationalistic position to faith.

We may describe pietistic rationalism as determination to come successively closer to God through prayer, Bible reading, and the study of devotional literature, which assist people to be stronger in faith. Nevertheless, the concern for a prophetic church in the world is, I think, a lesser role. Faith becomes an individual and personal behavioral pattern, disconnected from the world and from an integrated and united church.

However, in my understanding of stewardship, faith is about something understood, explained, and practiced within a community of believers. Private spirituality is thus problematic in a prophetic church if it just serves the individual rather than building up the identity of the church as a united body.[4]

PROTESTANT ETHICS

According to Weber, the Protestant work ethics above all implies a calling to work that underscored the performing of duty in worldly matters, and in contrast to monastic asceticism, as a way to salvation.[5] Women at home also found salvation through carrying out their duties in the home. There is no distinction or moral evaluation between different tasks, since it was the actual performance of obligations, inclusive of obedience to persons of authority, which had a divine worth. The modernization of religion, as in Protestantism, implied thus that the rational observance of laws and regulations (traditional) is now replaced with a strict observance of a calling to duty to work (as hard as possible one would presume).

The powerful conviction of a calling as obligation to God conflicted on numerous occasions with questions about community, peace, justice, and love, and are most noticeable in connection with missionaries' conscious calling as tasks for life. In television documentaries and stories about children of missionaries, we have sometimes heard how older mission pioneers were forced to leave their children at home or in remote boarding schools. Despite opposition from children, who in later life had difficulty in understanding this betrayal, it has often been defended as an unavoidable sacrifice to remain faithful to God's calling. Certainly, missionaries helped many people on the mission field when they did not need to give time and attention to their own children, but this is a typical instance of Western globalization of results-orientation and efficiency-thinking, which I mean is used to legitimate one's own interest in growth and progress of the mission enterprise. The

---

4. Jonsson, *Att vara eller inte vara kyrka*.
5. Weber, *The Protestant Ethic*.

calling had to be officially legitimated from the top of the mission organization and the missionary did not need to take their own responsibility of the children they had received as gifts of grace.

RATIONALIZATIONS INTO NEW FAITHS AND GODS

As mentioned earlier, we have seen how power may be justified through reference to religion, culture, or ethnicity. Different faith perspectives and spiritual experiences receive much attention in postmodern society. They have basically one commonality: their special interest in the spiritual and charismatic sphere in contrast to real-world experiences. Ritual, feelings, commitment, and myths end up having a central role, and they are essentially a postmodern reaction to modern rationality with a hierarchically structured and bureaucratic church. However, there is still very much a faith community that is separated from the world.

The New Age spirits rely typically on various rituals and symbols, which are believed to function as the best means to personal wellbeing. Faith movements are more typically religiously pietistic in character and rely on the strength and quality of one's formulation of faith in the Bible as the only word of God. This is in contrast to trusting fully in the gifts, resources, and talents of grace already given to all people by God and to be used in a mutual responsibility and accountability (ecumenical stewardship).

The focus of this new postmodern spirituality is the reception of spiritual gifts intentionally and mainly for one's own edification. Conversely, there is little recognition of a prophetic church. This was why the Apostle Paul urged his congregation to strive for the "gifts of prophecy" (1 Cor. 14:1) rather than the gifts of the tongue, since one should serve others rather than oneself. This is a gift of grace because it is freely given by grace from God (*charismata*). The grace and love from God is the basis of peace, forgiveness, and reconciliation to be extended to others. In the economy of grace, we can thus treat all gifts and resources as income, which people as stewards have to account for as dispenses in mutual accountability.[6]

6. Jonsson, *Att vara eller inte vara kyrka*.

The Power of the West in the Economy of Grace

PROSPERITY RELIGION

The gospel of prosperity could be critically seen as a spirituality that emphasizes growth and personal success as emanating from religious activities and regular praying. This spirituality is a form of rationalized spirituality, which expects profit as a gift of grace from God. For these, God's kingdom becomes visible in the form of material riches and personal success.

The communities inspired by the gospel of prosperity are often termed as a "faith movement," as the riches come as a result of strong personal faith. It cannot be ignored that even established church denominations and mission organizations present similar characteristics, such as when the quest for visible and measurable results or the determination to establish new churches and congregations. Even modern stewardship is then narrowly understood as a way to generate money as quickly as possible in order to strengthen and finance its own organizations and activities.

Result-oriented growth, that is prevalent in large parts of the charismatic movement, underplays the church's social and welfare tasks and issues of peace and justice. This spiritual result-orientation takes for granted that it was through starting missionary enterprises (pioneer activities) that the modern evangelization and mission was implemented. In spite of its close relationship to pietism, there are differences in the sense that modern mission is perceived pretty much as a business-oriented enterprise. Pietism was most probably a growth of religiosity emanating from a bureaucratic culture because of its piety regulations. Today's modern spirituality is instead a result of activities leading to the number of conversions calculated. Various so-called evangelical movements often endeavor to fix concrete objectives for peoples or nations not yet reached. In this connection, it becomes important to systematically compile statistics of the number of adherents converted to the right teachings.

The concept "unreached areas" implies quite a narrow view of what the missionary commission is about, easily eliminating the ethical perspective of mission that includes the promotion of peace and justice for all. There is a certain risk when the missionary commission is thought to be chiefly about conquering new geographical

Institutionalization of Religion

areas; there is a great risk that solidarity work is left to other denominations when one's own results can no longer be shown.

If instead the missionary commission is interpreted from the stewardship model outlined above and relates mission to the ethics as portrayed in Jesus' teaching on the kingdom of God, it is difficult to formulate tangible and measurable aims.

CONCLUSION

The disintegration and the elaborate hierarchical structuring of different denominations with different doctrines and confessions would at least partly be the result of the Western belief in rationality, growth, and progress. This has probably also contributed to an image of God that is at the top of the hierarchy in order to created legitimacy of the power of the state as well as the church. It is of course also possible that this common and even secular image of the kingdom of God has contributed to hierarchical power structures in the institutional society at large. However, this contrasts with the prophetic identity of the church, which relates to the teaching of Jesus about another kingdom of heaven where peace, love, unity, and justice is manifested.

The various religious institutions, including the church of course, are further rationalized due to the pressure for growth and resources. They often keep two separate tracks: one for spiritual and another for social or educational works, which is due to the pressure for external resources and legitimacy from the secular society. There is also a great risk that religious fundamentalism and centralization of power will increase as a reaction to the increasing demands for secularism that wants to separate religion from politics.

The challenge of stewardship, based on the identity of the church in the image of the body of Christ should therefore have potential to promote a mutual responsibility across different confessions or doctrines of different churches. Also, here the stewardship model of servant-hood leadership and mutual responsibility would strengthen the prophetic role of a united church in relation to the demands for peace and justice.

6

The Sacralized Economy

It is important to recognize that the globalization of modern rationality and economics is not as secular as one may think. Even references to God are made in order to boost economic growth and get legitimacy for capitalism from religions. Western religion is now rapidly privatized and disintegrated from the public, although it may seem that religion is increasing in organizational growth and membership.

What I mean is that Western globalization and market economics is inspired by a typical charismatic rationality for growth and expansion, and that the accumulation of wealth may even be legitimated as a blessing from God. It further demonstrates that this Western and anthropocentric view in relation to the rest of the world has also received legitimacy from modern religion.

The modern and the sacred belief in economic rationality and progress have characterized much of the modern discourse in political economy, business, and management during the period of industrialization. Modern neoclassical economy appears then as a kind of inversion of God in Nature as observed by Linnaeus. Nelson argues that individual self-interest and a self-regulating market are then turned into a secular religion.[1] Thus, the business market is receiving legitimacy from religion in more or less the same way as the state.

1. Nelson, *Economics as Religion*.

This problem is somehow similar to the growth of new religions, sects, and churches that is contrary to what secularization theories have anticipated in modern societies. However, this growth happens not least in the so-called developing countries like Latin America and Africa and particularly in urban areas where belief in modernization is stronger, which I shall elaborate on later.

FAITH IN THE INVISIBLE HAND OF GOD

Early in 1530, the word "oeconomy" referred to the art of household management and the household of God, and only through science could atheism be confronted (sic). Thus, there was a kind of marriage between religion and science, which all rested on three assumptions:

1. Nature functioned like a well-oiled machine once invented by God. (Descartes, Galileo, and Newton who saw God as an omniscient mechanic in fact supported this.)
2. Nature was related to the economy of God.
3. Man was seen as an economist in the image of God.

What I have found through the study of Nelson and other critics on modern economics, is that in the historical review of various ecological ideas starting from 1700, industrialization is criticized for its narrow specialization, causing an alienation of scientists. There is also an attack on Christendom and Protestantism for its support of Western science, as it also alienated the human being and soul from the material possessions and the body. Nature was now seen to have its own law of God, and only humans had moral value, while animals and plants were to be utilized for human benefits only.

In 1749 "The Oeconomy of Nature," the thesis by Linneaus, became a pivotal work.[2] All species were given names, and the purpose was to find the hand of God in nature, as he saw that there was an organic system where all species had their own particular role for the benefit of human beings. The system guaranteed there would be

2. Ibid.

enough food for everybody, and those humans had a particular role in creating balance as shepherds, and as such are stewards of God.

We can therefore see that in the family household the women occupied a central role as the economist, organizing the production and consumption, while still fulfilling the role as producer and consumer like other members. Consequently, it is modern industrialization that has contributed to the disengagement of the family household, and local economy run by women from the wider business market and politics.

The alienation of workers from their work, and from rural local society, caused by modern industrialization, will then create an opposite reaction from proponents of human inter-relations and social concerns. From this, I would also conclude that the subsequent failure of state-planned economies as well as a market economy has to do with excessive rationalization, alienating personal and mutual responsibility. The fall of the Soviet system in 1989 should, from this perspective, not be seen as a failure of socialism, but rather of an out-rationalization of morality, solidarity, and humanness.

Below we shall look first at the development of neoclassical economics and its principles of rationality. Particularly since the 1990s, economic globalization has raised a lot of criticism against neoclassical economics with its self-regulating market theory, which has come under severe attack from ethicists, environment activists, and theologians. Although many attempts are made to deal with the failures of the modern market economy and demand a new economic system, it is still based on the same basic faith in modern economics and the belief in modern rationality.

Therefore, it should be necessary to develop new and economic and ecological principles that will bridge the gap between both modern and traditional economics and cultures, but also between different political forms of modern industrialization such as planned economy, capitalism, or market economy. We shall come back to this in the concluding recommendations.

THE GOD OF THE MARKET

In referring to Worster, Robert Nelson makes a historical review of the main economic discourse since Adam Smith, and particularly a review of the Paul Samuelson's economics.[3] He shows with references to the old institutional school (Veblen) before the World War, and scientific management (Taylor) after the World War, and later the market mechanism after World War II, how the new American progressive economy has been motivated with almost religious convictions. In brief, it moves from strong government intervention and regulation to the free operation of the market mechanism.

Nelson departs from Luther and later Weber's *Protestant Ethics and the Spirit of Capitalism* when he shows how neoclassical economics is at least partly based on the Lutheran Doctrine of the Two Kingdoms and argues that social and economic growth in this world is part of God's will. State and church have two different mandates or callings: maintenance of creation and spiritual salvation. There is thus a separation between the secular and the sacred spheres.

Nelson states that classical economy is working through the "invisible hand of God" and refers to Adam Smith emphasizing that self-interest implies welfare for others. Rather than accumulate capital for the future, it should be spent in trading with other merchants. Gradually, the natural law of economics has, however, received greater and greater freedom and is now seen as the ultimate reality, with no further need for God.[4]

Marx later represented very different interests and personalities from classical economics, although still both believe in the new ultimate reality! He argued that conflicts between classes would in the long run overthrow the capitalist forces and establish a communist utopia, which will live together in harmony. A new world of abundance will not create any conflict and everybody will receive according to need, it was thought. All land and property should be owned by the state under a communist system of democracy. The state is now the good steward of Gods gifts and resources.

3. Nelson, *Economics as Religion*.
4. Ibid.

Domination by capitalist forces will alienate workers from their own production rather than being controlled and created by them. This will not only create poverty but also social ills and crime, it was argued.

Later Samuelson represented, according to Nelson, American progressivism. He is far more skeptical of the role of government regulation favored by Marx and Keynes, although all of them believe in the law of economic forces (materialism). Marx and Keynes differ on the future perspectives on how the new ultimate reality will come. Marx ideas build on a conflict perspective and a final catastrophe before the communist utopia of abundance, while Keynes looks forward to gradual but great changes, which "indeed has already begun." Marx was a materialist, but his utopia is not less spiritual in his belief in progress and wealth for all. Keynes is more scientifically rational in bringing a new world of abundance. Keynes road to heaven is capitalism rather than communism, but both "religions" seem to bring a utopian world of harmony and health for all, presented in spiritual dressing. It is however quite clear that both of them were reaching for heaven on earth.

Samuelson presents the Scientific Revolution of Fredrick Taylor as a gospel of efficiency and a secular awakening. Leading progressive Gifford Pinchot, a close advisor to Theodore Roosevelt, declared that his lifetime mission was "to help in bringing the Kingdom of God on earth" and "baptized with the holy water of reform." The United States was said to be a "nation with the soul of a church."[5]

Nelson also writes that the previous religious awakenings have taken on a secular form like the gospel of efficiency, and today environmentalism could be seen as a new wave with its special strategy and planning in opposition to the former religion of economic growth and efficiency. However, it is still like reaching for a heaven on earth.

He then states that after World War II in 1948 Samuelson had explained that this gospel of market mechanism, that is supposed to be far better than government allocation and what the direction

5. Ibid.

of central market institutions will be able to allocate, through regulating the pricing of necessary goods. The perfect market theory, although very unrealistic in practice, is supposed to bring both access to goods and fair prices through full competition.

In the idea that modern economics is a religion is also a lack of scientific evidence for any perfect market purely based on economic self-interest. The assumptions of this belief are also very reasonable, as there is the unrealistic condition of access to full information about available choices in the market.

The new modern economics with privatization made it also inefficient to make any comprehensive and long-term plan. The new and global market force replacing much of the role of national politics therefore also need to receive support from "higher" values represented directly by the consumers.

One could therefore assume that justice for the weak is best achieved through market mechanism, although the reality looks grim. At the end, he realizes that his belief in common values and the firm is soon replaced with more economic desires and individual self-interest. The injustice and social deprivation is not being reduced as foreseen through the gospel of efficiency and economic growth. The affluence of material goods and welfare does not seem to bring heaven down to earth.

THE CHICAGO SCHOOL OF ECONOMICS AND THE MORAL COMMUNITY

What happens in the 1960s and onward is known as the Chicago school of economics originating from Frank Knight, who inspired such economists as Henry Simon, Milton Friedman, Ronald Coase, and Gary Becker. The Chicago school could be seen as a belief in the rationalization and privatization of the market as a result of the emerging local empowerment and general critique against top-down structures and government involvement. The market consists of individual actors exerting more self-interest, but without the invisible hand of God", that was suggested by Adam Smith. Ethics according to Milton Friedman is to act according to the owners of property, the shareholders. Freedom becomes freedom of the market and the market mechanism is extended into political, social, and religious arenas as well.[6] The marketing of services and immaterial goods are also treated any commodity, which can receive a price and be sold or bought in a market. Examples are human organs and the rights to carbon dioxide pollution. Many of the Chicago economists have recently received the Nobel Prize in economics and are very frequently referred to in scientific articles. Gary Becker received his prize for the studies on economic behavior in marriage and divorce, which demonstrate an expanding belief in an economic rationality even outside the market arena into politics, religion, and family.[7]

NEW INSTITUTIONAL ECONOMICS AND MARKET REGULATION OF ETHICS

The Chicago School of modern economics continued in the same way as new institutional economics, which was first developed by Ronald Coase and today has had a major impact on the economics profession, which is being spread as part of the Western globalization of market economics. Douglas North who received the Nobel Prize in economics in 1993 considers Coase's works as a connection of neoclassical economics with institutional analysis. However, the new institutional economics is distanced from the old institutional school that instead involved cultural and religious influences on economics, as explained also in historical studies by Max Weber. The old school assumed a stronger role of the state while the new school assumes voluntary and social or ethical contracts and rules between market actors.

Douglas North brought to light the problem of transaction costs and imperfect or asymmetric information, which explain the failure of the perfect market. The new deregulated market system without the old government institutions created a need for new institutions and norms such as codes of conduct and agreements

6. Friedman, "The Social Responsibility."
7. Nelson, *Economics as Religion*.

as rules for players in the market arena. Joseph Stieglitz who got the Nobel Prize in 2001 has particularly drawn attention to what he calls "perfect ignorance," which has characterized neoclassical economics for a long time. The cost of transaction and imperfect information was largely neglected and just treated as externalities. The complicated system of decision-making, information, culture, and leadership was neglected in what he calls the "competitive paradigm."

Particularly since the 1990s, there has been a growing movement to recognize a larger role for cultural influences. Modern business firms are also shaped by the contents of its belief systems, and leadership quality and inspiration affect the results as well. In addition, once culture comes into the picture there is short distance to the use of religion to boost the growth of the market.

The new developments with economic globalization and the new institutional economics came when the assumption of moral behavior was previously taken for granted. Now radical changes in society, with an ever-expanding new system of global regulations have implied a huge dissolution of trust.

Nelson concludes that the new institutional systems of the market cannot replace a trustworthy citizen, and therefore the crucial question whether is to instill a belief system that ensures trustworthy behavior. What he suggests is to abandon the view that the corporation is a decision-making entity, but rather a corporate ecology still allowing for individualism. The corporation is not primarily a legal entity but a set of "contractual relationships" or "implicit contracts."[8]

My conclusion of these suggestions is, however, that the longing for trust and moral behavior runs the risk of being outrationalised" into contracts and regulations of some sort. The main argument of my analysis so far is, however, that the processes of rationalization with formal or implicit contracts lead to an ignorance of the common faith in social, mutual, and common responsibility, as assumed in the model of stewardship we have suggested. I shall come back to the corporate social responsibility (CSR) in

8. Ibid.

other chapters, and then suggest a wider perspective of identity and purpose for business than the belief in self-interest that has been discussed in this chapter.

THE ECONOMIC RELIGION OF THE UNITED STATES

Nelson refers to theologian Michael Novak when he comments that American welfare and the national unity culture might be regarded as the "church" of a state religion, which is not Christianity or Judaism. In referring to Bellah, he states instead that it is a "civic religion," which is almost like the nation itself.[9] This is held together with reference to God, although Christianity is not a state religion. A religious economy with the "gospel of efficiency" and progress has then replaced the identity of a national church in order to provide legitimacy for the State.

Economics as religion does not seem very different from the papal system of salvation rights offered in exchange for money to finance the St. Peter's Church of Rome. In the same vein one could perhaps now consider the payment of emission rights as a way to out-rationalize the obligation for all to save the creation. There is thus much to support the idea that the belief in the market is almost a religion in itself, which is sacred in the sense that it cannot be questioned, like the charismatic type of authority in religious sects.

My view is that such an understanding follows in principle the idea of Enlightenment that came with Newton physics. The previous conception of God as an intervener in everyday life was now replaced with a God of natural science. Science itself has replaced religious faith. Adam Smith's invisible hand in economics was a direct consequence of Newton's revolution in natural science. Darwin and Marx perhaps came to replace Newton and Smith with an evolutionary approach, both of their theories implying competition between species and classes, and now between suppliers and consumers. In addition, "the survival of the most competitive" may in the new civic religion and business market be accepted as God's

9. Ibid.

natural law, although it may have disastrous moral consequences. And the church of humanity is out-rationalized.

PROTESTANT ETHICS AND CAPITALISM

In a similar way Protestantism have given legitimacy to business capitalism as well as the State. The economic self-interest in a narrow sense became with the rising Protestantism an obvious goal for the business corporation. Weber showed, for instance, that among Protestants and particularly Calvinists there was a greater interest in business entrepreneurship than with Catholics. Typical was the shift from feudalism to the rational differentiation of business from the household economy. Therefore, it became even legitimate for the capitalist to retreat from social responsibility and it became a private concern or something for the church to take care of. The vocation itself became, under Protestant ethics, a calling from God, and under the influence of the prevailing hierarchical structures the loyalty and faithfulness to the employer became an act of piety. Being a capitalist was then seen as a divine calling, even superior to the worker's calling.

This reflects in my view the modern understanding on stewardship, which has been criticized for its superiority and exploitation of natural and human resources according to the Western and anthropocentric view of modern development. Stewardship became in Lutheran theology attached with the responsibility of the state and society for the creation, while the role of church was limited to salvation of the soul. Church stewardship was primarily understood as the collection of money from the church members in order to finance the expanding organization and its programs of the larger church administered by the clergy.

CONCLUSION

The challenge of a stewardship of grace tells us that all resources given by God are to be shared for the benefit of all in the global household. What this chapter has shown is that belief in God is used in order to receive legitimacy for privatization and capitalism with little regard to the identity of the church to be a sign of equality, peace, unity, and economic justice.

The prophetic identity of the church is therefore, I would say, out-rationalized. Here even war or a free market revolution can get wider support with references to God. The challenge of stewardship is a mutual responsibility rather than a competition between self-interested actors. The invisible hand of God assumed by Adam Smith has turned into the invisible hand of the market God. What we have noted thus is a kind of out-rationalization of the humanitarian and social aspects of business, when even institutionalization of ethical rules may give legitimacy.

The challenge of a responsible stewardship of resources is to widen the understanding of identity and purpose of business as well. Economic rationalism, market orientation, and narrow financial perspectives will otherwise create serious economic crises, where there are no reserves for future and common social needs, or ecological investments for coming generations.

Classical economics talk about a household economy, but modern economics seem to have lost this wider understanding of economy. Therefore, there would be a need to reintroduce the stewardship theory of management in business administration as well as ecological economics.

In the next chapter, I will demonstrate how the belief in a business and market-oriented rationality also has an impact on the institutions of the church.

7

Market Orientation of Religion

THE WESTERN GLOBALIZATION OF a market-oriented religion has also had an impact on the wider international church context. There is a lot of pressure for church growth in the East and South with a charismatic rationality and the planting of new churches and sects in Latin America, Africa, and Eastern Europe.[1] Therefore, there is a challenge for an ecumenical identity of stewardship with mutual responsibility and service in order to be a prophetic sign of unity, rather than a religious corporation demanding effective and charismatic leadership by the church leaders.

POSTMODERN RELIGIOUS CHANGES

The view of secularization in what is sometimes called postmodern society has come under attack, as religion in some societies is rapidly growing and multiculturalism is promoted in the society at large. The financial support for the church is, however, now gradually replaced with business-oriented approaches, as it becomes increasingly difficult to get aid and contributions to the church as a whole.

Religious changes in the era of globalization at the beginning of the new century has, according to most religious sociologists, taken a new direction: increasing interest in religion appears to

---

1. Chestnut, *Competitive Spirits*.

grow when it is privatized and not governed by the state, as has been the case in America particularly. Religion and culture in Europe is changed through a sort of mutation of memories, as religions and cultures such as Islam are mixed with Catholic and Protestant beliefs and cultures; this would form new constellations of religious and cultural identities.[2]

Therefore, it is not just a matter of modern secularization leading to reduced membership. It may even be a matter of spiritualization as a reaction to the modern secularization in Europe.[3] Religious globalization thus would offer a typical multireligious situation. Nelson also states that many people are in fact searching for religious alternatives to Christianity, coming for instance from Islam, Eastern religions or the New Age spirituality.[4]

As to the future development of the role of the church as a moral communion and demonstrating unity and peace, it should become imperative to search for a wider and common identity of churches and religions. The dominant public view about religions seems otherwise to be that the multiplicity of different religions and cultures, through postmodern relativism, out-rationalize the common moral identity of peace, unity, and justice.

Since the 1990s, religious sociologists have borrowed much thinking from the Chicago school of economics in the study of churches in America, which are seen to grow when adopting the market mechanism in the provision of religious services. Many say that in states with a strong private sector religious services are offered according to what is popularly expected, and so they attract members.[5] These members act more as consumers of religious service rather than as a mutually responsible community of believers. Mainline Protestant denominations as well as Catholic churches with closer affiliation to the state are therefore losing members.

---

2. Davis, *Religion in Modern Europe*.
3. Woodhead and Heelas, *Religion in Modern Times*.
4. Nelson, *Economics as Religion*.
5. Warner, "Work in Progress."

Market Orientation of Religion

Similar developments are also clear in Latin America,[6] East Africa, and the Nordic countries as well, where the Lutheran state churches and the mainline Protestant denominations are losing members to evangelical churches, sects, and movements. In the new churches, there is also a clear dichotomy between the spiritual and the social or humanitarian spheres. In general, free market-oriented churches are critical to government regulation and mainline churches and prefer the charismatic type of spirituality and leadership, which promotes a kind of business-oriented entrepreneurship in marketing the gospel. They may compete for new members with promises of a new heaven and God's saving action in life here and now, in contrast to traditional religion that has largely accepted that their fate in this life is the will of God.

The interesting question, which Chicago sociologists and economists have shown in their studies, comes from Nelson: where is the limit for self-interest and greed? The new modern religious movements can, however, also be seen as further secularized, as there is a belief in prosperity and visible growth in new church organizations, new members, and new and expensive church buildings. The new prosperity religions seem to say it is the will of God to apply private self-interest, and that economic growth is the result of strong faith. Adam Smith's assumption of self interest and the invisible hand of God appear to be applied not only to business but to religion also. As a result of urbanization and belief in scientific knowledge, it has for a long time been noted that religious faith has weakened in modern societies. As a result of postmodern changes with privatization of a diversity of interests and cultures it is, however, now being argued by religious sociologists that there is a global growth in new religious movements, sects, and churches. Faith communities act in a free market of competing spirits due to deregulation from the state in spiritual matters.[7]

Partly as a reaction to religious fundamentalism or extremism, it is often argued in secular societies that religion must be separated from the public sphere of politics, science, and education. If viewed

---

6. Chestnut, *Competitive Spirits*.
7. Ibid. See also Beyer, *Religion and Globalization*.

from an institutional perspective, it might therefore be more correct to talk about an increasing segregation and fragmentation in the society at large. What happens is namely that the growth of new churches, religions, and sects are increasingly assuming different identities and even withdrawing from their prophetic identity in the world.[8]

As explained above, secularization also takes place *within* the church, which some religious sociologists call an "internal secularization."[9] Chaves writes about the declining power of religious authority while my focus is more on the declining prophetic and united identity of the church and religion as a result of institutional disintegration. This may also happen as management and economy is not related to theology or faith. It is therefore usually accepted that churches, religions, and other nonprofit organizations particularly in the Western world can adopt popular management models as those being applied in business corporations, public education, etc. It is also without much reflection that modern economic rationalities based on individual self-interest may contrast with the identity of the church; this is a matter of justice and mutual solidarity. Even spirituality may then be treated as a matter of self-interest.

My assumption is thus that the free market of religious movements may lead to the search for measurable growth and new market shares, rather than a prophetic church that is seeking to witness for unity, peace, and justice in the world.

EXPANDED PRIVATIZATION

According to proponents of neo-liberalism, deregulation of the market is preferred. The market "players" should be free to choose according to private choice and preference, which will then bring about global economic growth and welfare for all. There is similar development of modern religion.

However, our ecosophic worldview and the philosophy of stewardship are based on the assumption of mutual responsibility

8. Davies, *Religion in Modern Europe*.
9. Chaves, "Intraorganizational Power."

and interdependence of spiritual, political, ecological, or social concerns. The so-called postmodern society implies a new and more intensive phase in the process of rationalization, which now is fragmented, private, and individualistic. In the same way, it is logical to suppose that the church's ecumenical and united identity risks being out-rationalized. As a consequence, the church's prophetic role, and her social criticism, may have a reduced significance as a result of globalization. Independent and determined individuals do not have control; instead, power is located in rationalized categories such as authorities, organizations, and companies.

DIVISIONS BETWEEN THE SACRED AND THE PROFANE

This process of rationalization in postmodern society is also the driving force in the typical division between the sacred and the profane. Moral concerns, which also exist outside the religious bodies, are therefore not considered to be any unique feature of churches and religions. According to sociology of religion with a postmodern outlook, there is a kind of resemblance between religious organizations and commercial enterprises, in terms of supply and demand.

This popular school of thought in religious sociology regards religious character mainly as transcendent, and the founder as having private religious interest to acquire as many followers and attendees as possible. This is comparable to an institution that offers various services and activities for its members spiritual needs.

The growth of private spirituality and the expansion of various sects and faith movements indicate that the older theory of secularization, going on mainly outside the church, is outmoded. This new postmodern and free market idea makes it, however, difficult for the church to act as the stewardship model suggests, having a prophetic role in the world to be manifested in the unity of the body of Christ. It is also problematic as the social responsibility within the church may be further separated from its wider identity of having a prophetic role to speak critically in favor of a real peace and economic justice in the world.

MANAGER OR PROPHET?

The question is what significance this has for the development of church leadership and the role of power. In traditional and modern societies, it has been legitimate to refer to Episcopal authority as God's representative. The clergy hold an office considered superior to lay responsibilities. From the stewardship perspective, however, the typical traditional and modern rationality is problematic since it takes hierarchical authority and control more or less for granted. In the postmodern perspective, control and authority is rather converted into a horizontal or even bottom-up relation. However, we have seen such relations develop from the idea of the free market approach, where the church is treated as one of the actors or players providing spiritual needs in a marketplace.

With reference to the stewardship view, the spiritual needs are instead seen as means of grace, instituted in order to manifest the church as a wider community of love and care. Stewardship presumes a common mission, task, or calling to manifest a message. Therefore, it is wider than the more technical role of service management. In times of crisis when it is necessary to realize more profound changes in society, particularly regarding the importance of peace and justice in order save humanity at large, the prophetic role of the church is necessary. This can raise stronger awareness that all people have a mutual responsibility and accountability to use their talents and resources rather than to expect solutions from the top or through market competition.

CONCLUSION

The challenge of stewardship is to manifest a common identity of peace, love, and unity in world society as a whole. Consequently, this should also be shown in the institutional development of the church as well as other religions. In the pluralistic modern society, the secular view is that religion is private, which does not really allow the church to be prophetic in the wider society. With hierarchical and disintegrated structures and secular management strategies, this is a contradiction.

The challenge for a united church is to revisit the original meaning of stewardship of grace in order to realize that the various denominations and sects should not be competing for growth and the right confession in order to attract new members. The challenge of stewardship based on a united and prophetic identity is, rather, to be directed towards local congregations to widen ecumenical and interreligious cooperation. The challenge of stewardship is also to see social responsibility as an integrated part of the mission and faith of the church rather than something that is out-rationalized from a spiritual identity.

8

Towards an Ecosophic Economy

IN THE PREVIOUS CHAPTERS, I have tried to explain the impact of Western globalization in the world at large. There has been considerable disintegration, conflicts, injustice, and centralization of power, which weaken prophetic identity and the ecumenical unity of church as well as religion in the witness for peace, justice, and unity. I will now present some further challenges of stewardship for a multicultural world. First of all the ecosophic worldview presented in the first chapter will be used to explain the interdependence in a stewardship of grace. We can therefore also treat it as an ecosophic economy as the different spheres of spirit, humanity, and nature are seen to be interdependent.

The enlightened self interest seems to be the new business ethics instead of the invisible hand of God. Social responsibility and sustainability appear to be interpreted in an instrumental way to promote economic growth in the long run. Religion, human relations, and ethics have in neoclassical economics been treated as externalities, but it in modern economics it may now be re-embedded in the networks of business relations as means and instruments for increasing profits rather than as an overall purpose and identity.

In contrast to this Western and egocentric view I will further elaborate on the stewardship philosophy from an ecosophic worldview. This helps to integrate the modern institutional structure and the concept of rationality within the wider externalities of the

Towards an Ecosophic Economy

cultural and religious identities. The need for social and cultural embeddings of economy makes it necessary also to integrate religion, but at the same time pay attention to the new concerns of multiculturalism and pluralism in order to bridge the tensions between modern and traditional identities.

In doing so we have to look at the diversity of cultures, ethnicities, religions, as well as nature as resources and opportunities for mutual interest and responsibility of all rather than as externalities or constraining factors to the modern and disembedded economy. Therefore, modern culture is of course a great resource with its new technology and traditional culture and its respect for local and social integration. The main concept of mutuality is ultimately guided by solidarity with all people of the world and also with future generations. Thus, we can talk about an economy of a wider household including the world society at large. However, this idea is of course not altogether new and we have to reintegrate tradition as well.

THE HOUSEHOLD ECONOMY

As we already noted in the introduction, the basic meaning of household economy and stewardship goes back to the ancient Greek word of *oikos* meaning "house" and *nomos* meaning "law." Today, economy is basically used as a financial concept, while I will use the household idea of economy with a much wider meaning including for instance social, human, spiritual, and cultural resources. This concept of economy was used even for the whole humanity when it was spoken of as *oikoumene* and economy of God as a plan of salvation.[1]

Further, economy was understood as strategies to "build up" (*oikodomé*) develop and maintain the community (*koinonia*). If the family or the global communities do not feel mutually responsible for the "building," it will affect the household of common resources. It is a question of participation, identity, and unity. To have an

---

1. See Brattgård, *God's Stewards*; Brodd, "Stewardship and Ecclesiology"; Meeks, *God the Economist*; Hall, *The Steward*; Reumann, *Stewardship and the Economy of God*; Stählin *Mysteriet*, Brander, *Människan*.

identity is important in all cultures and particularly in traditional cultures, where social embeddings are stronger than in modern societies. Therefore, we shall revisit the traditional understanding of economy as a household in an attempt to look for an integrated model for a multicultural and multireligious context. Rosser refers for instance to the Japanese model of society as a "household" or "family groupism" in explaining some of the trends within a "new traditional economy."[2]

As we shall see below there are indications that traditional economic identities within various religions or cultures are based on similar concerns[3] and we will find that also traditional culture and religious knowledge has something to contribute in this respect.

SPIRITUAL ECONOMY

In the rest of this chapter, I will review some earlier studies, which have been made on the economic rationality within various religions and cultures. The main question to be answered is then about the basic economic principle of a particular religious or cultural identity.

According to the modern Enlightenment since 1700 and onwards it is, however, assumed that religious faith is part of a traditional culture and different from scientific reason and economic rationality, which instead is part of a modern culture, and should be excluded from politics and economy. The German sociologist Max Weber became in the early 1900s on the other hand very famous for his works in religious sociology when he demonstrated that modern Protestantism gave legitimacy to capitalism. Recent developments around 2000 indicate also that the postmodern culture of individualism and private spirituality is strongly related to privatization and competition in a business market.

In order to find out how a spiritual economy shares resources I have briefly reviewed some of the literature on religions and cultures, which were considered to be relevant in this context.

2. Rosser, "The New Traditional Economy."
3. Wilson, *Economics, Ethics and Religion.*

Towards an Ecosophic Economy

1. How is economic thought presented in traditional and local religions and cultures?
2. How does religious thought appear in modern economics and cultures?
3. Is it possible to find a mutual understanding for a multicultural global economy and a sustainable society?

We have in the previous chapter stated that religion has particularly in the past played an important role in understanding nature and economics (Linnaeus, Smith, Weber, Worster). At the same time, religious and cultural studies demonstrate elaborate thinking on economic thoughts where God is even imaged as an economist.[4] These studies are commonly about the revelation of God in natural reality, human experience, economics, and in particular about the household of God (*oikos*) as well as the worldwide church and humanity (*oikoumene*).

I will first approach some of the studies on the concept of economics revealed in major religious doctrines, which can tell us something about the economic principles of a "household."[5]

JEWISH ECONOMICS

The Ten Commandments of the Old Testament that were received by Moses and to be followed by the Israelites are included in the holy book of Torah and include ethical laws that were part of a contract (covenant) with God. Interest was, according to Torah, not allowed to be taken from the poor. The trading partners had to set fair prices, be honest, and follow declared regulations. In the Jubilee Year (every 1000th year), all debts were written off. In this way, a balance in the economy was achieved and the poor had a chance to start afresh and so have a new life.

All property is according to Torah seen as belonging to God, viewed as the provider of all good things. Both trade and government regulations are to be established in order to protect the

---

4. Meeks, *God the Economist*.
5. Wilson, *Economics, Ethics and Religion*.

disadvantaged. Pure self-interest is therefore not allowed. Instead, there are regulations to promote mutual financial help and the members of synagogues are expected to give tithes in supporting the religious services and the poor people. The economic order is expected to reflect the divine order.

However, this is according to religious law but in the business economy today the thinking about perfect information, the concept of equilibrium and efficiency is equal to modern Western economic rationalities.

In traditional Judaism the household is seen as the basic unit (Mishnah) including an extended family/community, where there should be social equality between households and no hierarchy exist. The prices are determined in the market although fair prices are the rule. Real wealth is seen as received by God and it cannot be accumulated or consumed unless being subject to giving of tithes in order to support the temple and the poor. Transferring resources from one land to another with scarcity would please God. Man should act rationally in order to improve effective use of resources for the sake of all in the long run.

Wilson states that there are parallels in Talmudic literature with Adam Smith's moral philosophy that assumes that "an operational balance exists which harmonizes individual efforts with the interests of society."[6]

Thus, we can conclude that the religious economy of Judaism departs from an understanding that property belongs in principle to God, which means that excess resources are to be mutually shared. The giving of tithes is a practical law in order to support this understanding. The traditional understanding of economy is about mutual dependence on resources and it is related to the family and the social community and there is no hierarchy.

CHRISTIAN ECONOMY

Wilson concludes that biblical Christianity shares much of the Old Testament's history and teaching with Judaism and Islam. On the

---

6. Ibid., 52.

concept of economy, there are several references to stewardship in the New Testament and it is very similar to Judaism about helping the poor, although the teaching of Jesus is far more radical as it applies to the whole world. It is also similar to Judaism, stating that all things are created and given by God. The gifts given by the grace of God are to be used for good things for others, but not accumulated just for oneself. There was however, a clear difference as Jesus in a story about good stewardship condemned saving money or property without trying to get interest or return. However, the story was a parable in order to encourage a kind of entrepreneurship, so as to make good use of the talents and the grace received by everyone from God. Sharing with others in need is then important as well as saving for future needs.

There is a difference from Judaism as Jesus proclaimed a mission to other people, and according to the New Testament, he removed the boundaries between all different ethnicities like Jews, Greeks, heathens, and other people outside Israel. The Torah was to be applied only to the Israelites. The Christian concept of stewardship proclaimed mutual sharing, responsibility, and accountability, not only within Christian communities but also within the wider humanity (*oikoumene*).

Based on similar arguments from Meeks, Nelson, Wilson, and Skolimowsk, the Christian doctrine of Trinity relates to economy as well as ecology. It stresses the same kind of mutuality between Father, Son, and Holy Spirit, which include nature, humanity, and spirit. The economics can thus not be separated from religious identity, as material goods are also needed to fulfill the will of God. In referring to Meeks, it is further underlined that even the doctrine of the church (ecclesiology) is explained in economic terms. *Oikos* and *oikonomia* means access to livelihood and God's household. Access to livelihood comes through market relations. I would even admit that market economy is inevitable, but a market society is undesirable as social, political, or spiritual relations will then be forced into narrow financial terms of supply and demand or into measurable categories.[7]

---

7. See Meeks, *God the Economist*; Nelson, *Economics for Humans*; Wilson, *Economics, Ethics and Religion*; Skolimowski, *Ecological Humanism*.

The Power of the West in the Economy of Grace

My conclusion on Christian economic identity is that it rests basically on the understanding of *oikos* and *oikonomia* (stewardship). All people have received different gifts of grace from God, which are both natural and spiritual, and are to be used for the benefit of all. There is mutual responsibility and accountability for the use of resources in society, within the church as well as in relation to other religions and cultures. In the New Testament (Matthew 25) there are illustrative stories told by Jesus that presents the essence of stewardship with mutual responsibility for the poor and marginalized as our accountability to God.[8]

The Western belief in rationality has led to modern capitalism as well as communism, both of which separate religion from economy. It is, however, interesting that even the communist state in the former Soviet needed the Orthodox Church in order to get legitimacy for its power and politics.

ISLAMIC ECONOMICS

Islamic thought on economics stresses, however, the traditional interrelatedness between religion and economy. The discussion concerns rather what comes from Choran and what comes from Sharia law or even Western economy and globalization. Islam is seen as an alternative to both communism and capitalism and a way out of underdevelopment or a way to restore classical successes of Islam during its first century. In Islam, trading has been considered important as Prophet Mohammed was a trader and gave a lot of ethical teaching in the Koran, while Judaism and Christianity considered production more important.

Wealth in Islam is considered a means to serve God and humanity and not an end in itself. It is not a problem to be rich but how the property was acquired and how it is being used is the main challenge. What is important is that all should have enough although not equal. Those who have more should share with others (stewardship). Private ownership is the natural state of affairs. The prohibition of "riba" (interest) is central and means not to

8. Brood, "Stewardship and Ecclesiology."

take interest when it causes transfers of assets from poor to rich. Debtors should be treated with leniency rather than exploitation. In Western neoclassical economy, interest is regarded as reward for deferring consumption. Muslims however are not encouraged to hoard but to spend money provided by Allah for the benefit of his followers. Another important concept of economy applied is "ibar" (Ibn Khaldun), which both in Arabic and Hebrew means bridging, passing on, over, through, or beyond to historically internal events and bridging between spiritual and material. Culture means the social interaction of men in submitting themselves to the will of God and to understand God one must also study economic transactions. Two different economies are recognized, the primitive farming and the civilized trade and industry (civil society).

Islamic economic thought assumes a personal responsibility for all Muslims of the resources entrusted to them, and there is an obligation on resource owners to hear the grievances of those affected by what is done in their name. Investors must take active part in management and the proper use of their investments.

From these doctrines, we can conclude that Islam does not separate religion and economy in the same way as Protestant religion and Western economic culture. It seems that classical economic thought based on the principle of *oikos* and stewardship is largely the same as with Christianity. It stresses also a mutual responsibility for resources entrusted to them by God. The ban on interest implies instead that the mutual responsibility and accountability at the same time means a mutual benefit from the profit resulting from the investments of partners.

Modern Islamic market institutions have, however, as we shall see later, implied a more rationalized economy, which means a disconnection between investor and the trader. The financial institution receiving savings and investments takes over the role of the investor and the risk in forming the partnership (*musharakah*).

The Power of the West in the Economy of Grace

AFRICAN UBUNTU

African cultural and religious views on economics and globalization have recently been referred to in the ecumenical consultations of the World Council of Churches on Poverty, Wealth, and Ecology, for instance. There are a number of local cultural concepts here that are put forward as a new approach to discuss alternatives to modern economics. *Ubuntu* (humaneness) is a Zulu word with its origin in Southern Africa, describing the awareness of community, mutual commitment, and care among community members. A person with ubuntu is open and affirming to others, knows that he or she belongs to a greater whole. Ubuntu does not mean that people should not enrich themselves, but is it for the purpose of the wider community? Ubuntu is seen as one of the founding principles of the republic of South Africa. In Zimbabwe, the equivalent word to ubuntu is *unhu*.

Another word is *ujamaa* (life in community) which was popular in Tanzania during the time of Nyerere and described nationwide settlements in rural villages. Ujamaa comes from the Swahili word for "extended family" or "family hood." Characteristic is that a person becomes a person through the people or the community, where cooperation and collective advancement are the rationale of every individual's existence. Distribution of wealth should occur horizontally rather than vertically. Everyone should work for the community and for oneself.

THE NEW TRADITIONAL ECONOMY

A new but still traditional economy with mixed cultures is now emerging in countries with traditional cultures and religions in the East, although economic globalization from the West is still dominating. This takes place as a result of encounters between modern and traditional cultures, religions, techniques, and resources.

A global study of economic understandings in different countries in the East such as India, Iran, Pakistan, and China has demonstrated economic systems inspired by traditional as well as modern cultures.⁹ This is named new traditional economy. The theoretical support for this new system comes from the history of economics and the research made already in 1944 by Karl Polanyi.¹⁰ He sees this economy as "socially embedded." Rosser also means that the new traditional economy might be viewed as a reaction against the globalised conflict theory presented in the "The clash of civilizations and the remaking of world order."¹¹ The new traditional economy thus combines the modern and traditional and religions play a key role. My understanding of Huntington is however very different from the popular view of religious fundamentalism, which is rather modern in the sense that religion (and ethnicity) is often being misused by politicians and others in order to gain power over resources and support.¹² Therefore, economic systems and business relations should have a central social role when it comes to conflict management, as the scarcity of resources and poverty is a root cause of violence.

CONCLUSION

The religious core principles on economy appear to be much the same in the religious books of Torah, Koran and the Bible as well as African and other traditional religions and cultures. All state that properties, goods, and resources do not belong only to some individuals, but are in principle given by God to be used by all the people (economy of grace). This means that resources are given for a responsible use to serve others and particularly the poor, apart from one's own needs and livelihood. All seem to recognize a formal private ownership, which, however, is based on the understanding of mutual responsibility, and accountability, which at the same time constitutes accountability to God. For Judaism and Islam the principles apply primarily to the respective religious community, while

---

9. Rosser, "The New Traditional Economy."
10. Polanyi, *The Great Transformation*.
11. Huntington, *The Clash of Civilizations*.
12. Meyer et al, *Institutional Structure*, 12–37.

The Power of the West in the Economy of Grace

New Testament Christendom applies the principles to the wider world society.

In referring to Asian and African cultures and religions, we can likewise see that the traditional cultures stress local and mutual sharing and cooperation. Private identity or participation is formed in relation to the wider society, which is different from modern economics disembedded from the social and cultural context. The Western understanding of religion and economy reflect, however, a typical dualism between sacred and profane spheres.

In this vacuum, there is a need for the ecosophic worldview outlined, which can integrate spirit, humanity, and nature as an economy of grace. This is also the case with the deeper understanding of stewardship, economy, and ecology, which is seen as a household.

9

The Reason for Faith in Modern Societies

MY CRITIQUE AGAINST THE Western modernization of narrow rationality and fragmented centralization leads me now to point to the concept of a common identity or faith for a wider rationality, that is, how to live the faith in deeds or how to develop institutional structures as signs of unity and peace.

The ecosophic worldview with ecological humanism introduced by Skolimowski[1] and outlined in chapter 1 can also contribute to a wider understanding about tthe division between religion and science in modern societies.

What has happened is science in modern societies has gradually relegated religion to the spheres of the sacred and private. However, we can also observe that science has become a kind of religion that gives legitimates the power of experts and researches, who are generally seen as objective and neutral. On the other hand, atheist movements (for instance, humanism) are sometimes identified as faith movements and even gather in religious places in order to strengthen their common spirit and fellowship. As I have written elsewhere in this book, there is an increasing internal secularization within modern church organizations. I would think that this development is a process of rationalization for the sake of legitimacy and

---

1. Skolimowski, *Ecological Humanism*.

support. Churches get legitimacy from the secular world when they apply modern scientific methods or economic rationality.

Therefore, what proponents for religious faith have to do is to admit that they cannot argue with scientific arguments or from a position of power, but appeal to the conscience of man and to its true mission of its identity as stewards of God. Faith is a matter of trust and not a matter of believing in modern scientific truth.

The roles of power have been justified by the weight of tradition, with no critical analysis of the damages they have caused, like support for slavery, war, and capitalism. Only when religion has shed these can it confess its true mission as a sign of peace, reconciliation, and justice. Religion cannot exercise its influence from positions of power. Therefore, disunity, disintegration, conflicts, and economic injustice, which do not reflect or manifest the identity of a united church as a sign of peace and justice for the poor and oppressed, also do not give credibility to the secular world.

FAITH AND REASON

If arguments for religious belief are made from scientific perspectives only, there would thus be no need for divine explanations. Instead, faith will become a private and subjective matter, also for those who defend religious belief based on an objective reality. If one regards the economy as an objective reality, this would therefore lead to a desire to dismiss even ideology and politics to the subjective sphere.

Postmodern philosophy has also declared that any common faith is superfluous; there is no objective and great narrative story to identify with. Philosophy, whose charge is seeking after truth, has accordingly abandoned this duty and confines itself to discussing how every person, each through their own edification, can find their own truth. From the stewardship perspective outlined, it should therefore be imperative to find something that can integrate the subjective reality of identity, and the objective realities.

One interesting theological-philosophical illustration of the essential interplay between faith and reason has emanated from

The Reason for Faith in Modern Societies

the Roman Catholic Church. The previous pope, John Paul II, who was also a philosopher, published an encyclical before the advent of the third millennium, entitled "Faith and Reason." He declared that reason and the human endeavor to find meaning in life presupposes a declaration of faith that is in accordance with divine evidence of the transcendental, which human beings could not know anything about. In brief, the message of this encyclical is a warning against the late-modern relativism, which threatens not only faith in a loving God but, above all, endangers reasonable human development and welfare. He warns that faith, understood as trust, should not be seen as opposed to knowledge but, on the contrary, it is a prerequisite for the development of a wider understanding.

He stated that an affirmation of faith engages the entire beings of people, including their will and intellect, which, in the framework of human communication, stimulates an openness for a deeper meaning:

My conclusion about the reason for faith, rather than belief in final, absolute, objective, or neutral truth, is it provides meaning for our search for further understanding. The action or deeds are not limited to means-end relations, but faith or trust in a merciful God provides love, spirit, and hope for sustainable and courageous actions for peace, unity, and justice. Institutional structures are not just means or instruments to implement goals. They are themselves signs or symbols that reflect identity and power. Scientific evidence is not always objective as it may depend on culture, norms, and interest of the researcher or the funding agency supporting or initiating the research.

This does not really challenge modern knowledge, as the assertion is that reason presupposes faith and strengthens it, as with all other knowledge and experience. A relativistic faith isolated from reason and practice and preoccupied with various doctrinal interpretations makes it impossible to grow in knowledge and to live by example.

The old emblem of the University of Uppsala in Sweden also illustrates the classical understanding of the connection between faith and reason. This juxtaposes truth (*verities*) between grace (*gratia*) and nature. In its classical sense, the Christian faith was about receiving God's grace and love, and reason belonged together with nature or God's creation. It is easy to have the impression that modernity has brought a rationalization of faith and is therefore interpreted from a secular point of view as belief in something that we do not know.

From the sociology of knowledge, we have come to know that also science is socially constructed. The objective reality is something that we know very little about, but the knowledge about objective reality is basically socially constructed.[2] But also belief is a knowledge that can be seen as socially constructed by the community of believers, or the community of theological researchers. For religion, this knowledge is a matter of belief and rooted in people's experiences, traditions, holy books, doctrines, etc. Faith then is more oriented to the future and points primarily to a vision, hope, and trust in peace, love, and unity.

LIVING THE FAITH

The discussion above suggests that there is a logical connection between faith and reason as one comes closer to a deeper understanding of what it means for the church to live the faith in deeds. It is this connection that is brought to light in the stewardship understanding of the prophetic identity of the church. This identity is thought of as limbs in a body that shall serve one another and as a sign of peace, unity and justice, which I developed in the preceding chapters of this book. It is also approximately similar to the way in which Dag Hammarskjöld, a former Secretary-General of the United Nations, developed his views on life's meaning in his posthumously published book, *Markings*. Here he also identified himself as God's steward in his prophetic diplomacy for world peace and specifically as an advocate for the young and new members of the United Nations in relation to the super powers of the Security Council.[3]

---

2. Berger and Luckmann, *The Social Construction of Reality*.
3. Hammarskjöld, *Markings*.

The Reason for Faith in Modern Societies

The conclusion that I would therefore draw is that there has been a repression of questions about living by example, allegiance to faith, and the meaning of being stewards of God, mainly because of the common separation between faith and deeds. This is caused by an out-rationalization of faith into the private sphere of religion and associated with a belief in the supernatural.

Most of the popular twentieth century literature on organizational theory and management studies seems, in my view, to be motivated by a belief in progressive rationalization of self-interest with little identification with the global household (bureaucracy, the administrative school, management, economic man). The stewardship of grace means instead that reason and rationality is necessary in order to live the faith in deeds.

STEWARDSHIP WITH THE OTHERS

The essence of the stewardship concept is that people have mutual responsibility and accountability in order to live the faith in deeds. Resources—spiritual, natural, or financial—are therefore, in principle, not for people to acquire, exchange, to invest in, and make profit from; instead, individuals are identified as both receivers and givers of *gifts* that have been given by grace to the wider community and for the benefit of all.

Partners in peace and development cooperation are, however, basically identifying themselves as givers *or* receivers, managers or owners of their own property. Their aid belongs to individual donors while the stewardship idea in principle implies a mutual sharing of all resources for the benefit of all.

However, according to the modern norms of public management, stewardship is mainly about how officials utilize the funds allotted either according to specific rules, assignments, and traditions or through the decisions and power of superiors. Also modern rationalizations of the stewardship concept have found its way even into the biblical language today. Good News Bible (a popular translation), for instance, translates "steward" with the modern word "manager."

With the same logic between faith and reason, the stewardship concept can also contribute to strengthening the mutual responsibility and mutual learning in contrast to institutionalized capacities, when responsibility may be transferred from actual people to particular roles, organizations, companies, and projects. This creates abstract, economic, and legal persons to whom employees, mediators, or conflicting parties are answerable but whom they do not know, and thus they are liable to feel a certain moral indignation.

RATIONALIZATION, FUNDAMENTALISM, AND SECTARIANISM

The separation of faith and reason is similar to the differentiation between the sacred and the profane sector, in religious as well as political and financial institutions. Some of the business ethics literature has also raised ethical objections to result-orientation and narrow profit motivation, which often stem from a concern of the survival and growth of companies or organizations.

The economic concern with results and the belief in the free market are reminiscent of religious fundamentalism that disregards identification with others. This leads to the draining of present-day resources that are required as a reserve for future generations. There is then a faith in the economy, which is focused on institutional symbols (money), which are disconnected from the real life world. Money, economic growth and share prices in the stock market become more attractive in comparison with the goods that people really need.

Business ethicists also draw attention to the fact that even business companies have wider social responsibilities in society instead of just being isolated within the private market. In emphasizing such principles, Robert Solomon suggests ethics such as social responsibility should not be isolated from business operations in general. He means that by their existence, companies have a wider responsibility to society. He stresses the importance of a holistic view of people, and he thinks that business ethics is about satisfying wider social purposes, instead of focusing on narrow and short-sighted institutional interests.[4]

This perspective is similar to our stewardship model as it takes a comprehensive view on faith and reason in order to live the faith in deeds. The invisible hand of God is therefore a matter of faith and reason and rationality is necessary for the manifestation of deeds.

CONCLUSION

The challenge of stewardship of grace, also seen from an ecosophic worldview of ecological humanism, emphasizes the interrelation between faith and deeds in a similar way as faith and reason. Reason must then be built on faith as trust rather than being separated from it. Therefore, faith is in important point of departure for motivating action and even more importantly to provide a basis for the manifestation of faith in institutional structures. Stewardship is different from modern management, as it does not make a division between faith and deeds. It implies that the manager also should live faith in deeds in order to demonstrate credibility and trust.

4. Solomon, *Ethics and Excellence*.

10

Peace and Justice in the Mysteries of Faith

IN THE QUEST FOR an ecumenical and interreligious identity and unity, the mystery of faith can be seen in the poetic language of religion, which can give a more unified understanding about the spirituality of different religions. The various religious doctrines and institutions could then be seen as incarnations or sacraments of a common spiritual identity.

The Christian mystery is about the crucified Jesus, seen as an incarnation or manifestation of the love of God for the world. The prophetic and united church is in a similar way seen as a "steward of the mysteries of the *grace of God*."[1] In a similar way, the church is to be a living manifestation of image of the body of Christ. It should therefore be necessary to seek a deeper understanding of the mystery of faith together with other religions as it was indicated in the chapter on multireligious economy of grace. This spiritual mystery goes far deeper than the rationalized identities of religions and cultures.

The mystery of Islamic religion is called Sufism and is, in a similar way, about the manifestations of the love of God.[2] In his paper "Sufism, Sufists—Sufist Orders" we can read:

1. Stählin, *Mysteriet*.
2. Godlas, "Sufism."

Sufism or tasawwuf, as it is called in Arabic, is generally understood by scholars and Sufis to be the inner, mystical, or psycho-spiritual dimension of Islam. Today, however, many Muslims and non-Muslims believe that Sufism is outside the sphere of Islam. Nevertheless, Seyyed Hossein Nasr, one of the foremost scholars of Islam, in his article "The Interior Life in Islam" contends that Sufism is simply the name for the inner or esoteric dimension of Islam.

After nearly 30 years of the study of Sufism, He also states that that in spite of its many variations and voluminous expressions, the essence of Sufi practice is quite simple. It is that the Sufi surrenders to God, in love, over and over; which involves embracing with love at each moment the content of one's consciousness (one's perceptions, thoughts, and feelings, as well as one's sense of self) as gifts of God or, more precisely, as manifestations of God.[3]

As we could see also from our brief review of some of the religious and cultural economic principles in an economy of grace, they manifest the love of God through the diversity of manifestations and gifts of God.

However, a popular understanding today is that religions and cultures are competing for influence and domination. It is then believed that, for instance, Islamic religion and culture will threaten Western Christendom and lifestyle. The reconciliation between religions is not just a matter of tolerance but, even more, the search for unity at a deeper and common level of peace and love, which is manifested through the grace of God (stewardship). It is quite simply a new paradigm of religious change that integrates the sacred and profane spheres, which is also the view expressed in the concept of sacrament, sign, or symbol. The theological studies I will refer to below point in the same direction, when the diversity of gifts is treated as gifts of grace.

3. Ibid.

A SPIRITUAL WHOLE

I understand then that peace, love, and unity can be seen as manifestations of the mysteries of the will of God, heaven, or a kingdom of God. Consequently, also the economic justice and sharing of resources between rich and poor is indeed a spiritual matter. Spirituality is different from the material, not because of its metaphysical nature, but it keeps together different fragments or parts of the whole.[4] Thus, spirituality is even a matter of sustainability. Ken Wilbur argues here that modern science is going through a paradigm shift from focusing on the particular measurability of the parts to understanding the wholeness (the holographic paradigm) as the invisible and primary reality. This is represented or manifested through the observable realities. Therefore, it cannot always be measured but just perceived through intuition or through the senses. To be together is about spirituality and mutual responsibility, but individual action and identity may lose the common identity within a larger whole.

GIFTS OF GRACE

We have stated repeatedly that stewardship from the perspective of mutual responsibility is the manifestation of the gifts of God for the welfare of all. There is thus a great challenge in multireligious and multicultural diversity to manifest the uniqueness of all into a spiritual whole. Stewardship does not give humanity the freedom to use all resources at our own will. It is not something mainly for the manager at the top of a hierarchy, but every human being is a steward and has received particular gifts to be used for the welfare of all, now as well as in the future.

The stewardship philosophy constitutes the identity and security of each within the wider context. This idea is conditioned by a view of humanity departing from the understanding that all human beings are equal and created in the image of God. As a consequence, it assumes a view of God that involves spirit, humanity,

---

4. Wilber, *The Holographic Paradigm*.

Peace and Justice in the Mysteries of Faith

and nature as suggested also in the ecosophic worldview. The dichotomy between the immanent and the transcendent has always been problematic for religion as the doctrine at the same time proclaims a holistic view that promises peace and justice already in this world, although not completely.[5]

There should thus be a great potential for stewardship thinking, which can demonstrate how the different religions and cultures can be seen as stewards of the mystery of the grace of God.

STEWARDSHIP AS MISSION

In connection with the interrelatedness of faith, ecology, and economy in stewardship, we can also see a major shift in the theology of Christian mission towards a more inclusive view of the meaning of mission including evangelism, diaconal and socio-economic development as well as the ecological concerns of climate change and environmental degradation. Characteristic of this transformation are what Woodhead and Heelas call the "religions of humanity," as spirituality is interpreted as located also within humanity and world.

Christian mission has often been connected with an imperialistic and sometimes colonialist attitude in order to expand the kingdom of God. However, many of the mainline churches in the West, and which we can also call "religions of humanity," have transformed their mission view from an entrepreneurial enterprise in foreign lands to a view of mission that is presented as being a sign of the kingdom of God in all contexts (the mission of God on six continents).

Broadly speaking this new development has implied that foreign church mission from the West has since World War II been handed over to self-governing churches in a similar way as colonialist regimes did after the formation of national governments in the former colonies. The new situation was outlined as mutual church relations or partnerships between interdependent churches with ecumenical relations. It is then argued that that the original task

---

5. Beyer, *Religion and Globalization*, 86.

of the church, as a community of believers is to be in mission. This modern historical development has been described in theological research as mission science or mission history.

More recent research describes a paradigm shift in the theology of mission.[6] As already stated in the introduction Bosch demonstrates thoroughly how the Enlightenment has affected modern mission and theology. The identity of the church is presented as the body of Christ. Mission is much broader than preaching the gospel in foreign lands. It is rather to be signs of the kingdom of God at home and it is the responsibility of all believers to live as light and salt. In this way, we can see how the Christian mystery is demonstrated in this new paradigm.

As a consequence of this discussion, the inclusive view of mission should therefore be synonymous with a stewardship of the grace of God. All religions therefore have a responsibility to pay greater attention to the mystery of grace and their deeper and wider identity as stewards of God.

THE WORLD AS THE BODY OF GOD

The rising concern for ecological and social justice issues and the development of eco-theology has in a similar way implied a shift towards a more inclusive view of God and the whole creation.

The theologian Sally McFague directs her critique indirectly against the Protestant view on stewardship, but criticizes more directly the neoclassical economic theory and the worldview, which has developed its own religion: consumerism.[7] She argues in a similar way as I have demonstrated that neoclassical economy is rooted in Protestant theology and ethics. These Protestant ethics give legitimacy to a growth of capitalism that could contribute to economic growth of the churches and its various works.

The calling and professional vocation as a work of piety according to Calvinist reformist theology was interpreted in such a way that it created legitimacy for modern capitalism. My view is

6. Bosch, *Transforming Mission*.
7. McFague, *Models of God*.

Peace and Justice in the Mysteries of Faith

that the pressure for economic growth is a result of neoclassical economics, and has implied an ever-increasing consumption has become a political motivational force to gain power, but which contrasts sharply with the pressure for sustainable development.

It is only now that we are beginning to realize that the pressure for economic growth threatens not only the ecology, but also the global survival of the poorest. What is needed, says Fague, is a "planetarium theology" that assumes an imminent and incarnated God, and for us to see the world itself as the body of God.

The consequences of this thinking should then be to understand economics from a new, ecosophic worldview that stresses mutual responsibility and where the various parts of humanity (*oikoumene*) constitute the limbs within a wider community.

Also in the ecumenical context, there has been a shift to new and more inclusive thinking. Lutheran World Federation, for instance, has since 1991 in Canberra tried to find new inclusive concepts and stressed that humanity is part of cosmos and created in the image of God. It is also now that influences come from Protestant ecumenical circles as well as Catholic and Orthodox theologians within the World council of Churches. The Greek concept of *oikonomia* comes into the discussion as well as the traditional theology of the Christian mystery. The ecumenical thinking has become central and the traditional doctrines of incarnation and sacrament have become important in order to highlight the view that humanity is created in the image of God and God's stewards. The mystery as the grace of God as both immanent and transcendent is receiving greater attention in theology.[8] The stewardship theology was again receiving attention and support at the Lutheran World Federation conference in Hong Kong 1997.[9]

---

8. Stählin, *Mysteriet*.
9. Brander, *Människan*.

THE ETHICS OF STEWARDSHIP AND MUTUAL RESPONSIBILITY

The stewardship philosophy itself is mysterious, as the spiritual and ethical imperative is an integral part of the management practice. However, the present debate about global ethics is the search for a separate definition of common values that have to be formalized and applied globally. There is then a risk that religious faith and traditional cultures will be marginalized in the drive for a sustainable globalization.

Grenholm and Kamengrazis conclude that universal ethics is controversial and is therefore critical to Hans Küng and his "Welt ethos," assuming that religions can contribute with a common ethics to guide. They suggest instead a critical dialogue will raise awareness of ethical aspects rather than universal declarations on ethics, which all cultures should be able to follow. There would be a great risk that the institution of ethical codes will be dominated by Western culture and the intellectual elite.

My conclusion is that the stewardship philosophy of mutual responsibility promotes critical dialogue where the ethical dilemmas as well as solutions in various contexts can be mutually agreed upon. The resistances to apply the stewardship philosophy are, however, rooted in the Western-oriented culture of individualism and relativism; therefore, a new ecosophic worldview is a great challenge.

STEWARDSHIP AND THE TRINITY

An exclusive view of religion may consider only a particular view of religion as true, but the modern pluralist view that all religions are true from their own perspective is problematic. It also excludes the view that there is only one God. Finally, it excludes the view of integration between religion and economy as it takes for granted the view that religion is a private matter.

Gavin D'Costa provides us, however, with a key to this dilemma that also reflects the *oikos* model of a divine economy (unity in diversity), and which is even more inclusive than the pluralist view,

Peace and Justice in the Mysteries of Faith

which only speaks of religions.[10] That is an interpretation of the doctrine of Trinity, which provides us with a link to other religions and humanity through the Holy Spirit. Through this model, God as creator is revealed through both nature and humanity through the Father. The divine economy (*oikonomia*) and the Trinity is reflected not only in Christianity but through the people of Israel, through Jesus and his disciples, and through the church, as well as other religions and humanity as a whole (*oikoumene*) with the help of the divine spirit of love in the heart of all.

D'Costa concludes that the narrow and partitioned management and economy in the modern world have occurred at great cost of humanity. Economy must be concerned with the livelihood and economic action that is supposed to serve the community at large. It is built on mutual responsibility and accountability between interlinked but free units within a Trinitarian understanding of God, rather than units within a hierarchy under a supreme God and king.

We can therefore conclude that God as economist, according to Meeks, and as a Trinitarian God, appears to be more or less the same. Both metaphors point indirectly to mutual responsibility and accountability as congruent with the accountability to God.

CONCLUSION

The challenge of a stewardship of the mysteries of faith is that an economy of grace submerges into a spiritual whole; that is, when the creation and the use and allocation of resources within the wider ecumenical community (*oikoumene*) is to be seen as a manifestation of God's love for all.

In theology and mission there is now a shift in paradigm towards a more inclusive, interdisciplinary, and eco-oriented theology as well as increasing ecumenical and interreligious discussions, which appear to be hold together by the view of nature, humanity, and spirit as a body of God and the church as the body of Christ. These body metaphors suggest that the world and the whole humanity, through their interdependencies and relations, are seen as

10. D'Costa, "Christ the Trinity and Religious Plurality."

limbs in the same body and which at the same time are manifestations of the love and grace from God.

The overall conclusion of our discussions in this book have departed from the understanding that the stewardship philosophy is not limited to the management and the financing of the organizational set up and its activities. Stewardship concerns a community of people being mutually responsible in the global household of various nationalities, religions, cultures, and ethnicities.

The challenge of stewardship is therefore particularly appropriate in bridging the sacred and the profane spheres of society and also within the church and religion as a whole. Stewardship highlights the prophetic identity of the church in the world. The disengagement between the two is mainly due to the process of rationalization and seen largely as internal secularization. As I have demonstrated in previous studies[11] the process of an instrumental rationalization typical of modern science and management leads to specialization, fragmentation, and differentiation, which eliminates mutual responsibility and a wider identity of the church. The stewardship principle puts the emphasis on the ecumenical identity of the church being the wider community of believers to manifest peace, love, and solidarity with all.

And the most important of all the ecosophic stewardship strategies provides a challenge to the contemporary structures of power and management, as all people in general are seen as stewards who have to take mutual responsibility to promote peace, justice, democracy, and equality of all. The identity of mutual responsibility and accountability cuts across the formal lines of authority and runs vertically as well as horizontally through the contemporary hierarchical structures of power and authority. Stewardship then means to serve one another according to the identity of church in the image of the body of Christ.

---

11. Jonsson, *Narrow Management*.

11

Concluding Analysis

IMPACT OF GLOBALISATION WITH CHALLENGES OF A PROPHETIC STEWARDSHIP

IN THIS CONCLUDING CHAPTER I will summarize some of the main conclusions I see as the root causes of conflicts from the impact of Western globalization. I will then elaborate further on the challenges of an ecumenical and ecosophic stewardship as signs for peace, unity, and justice in a multicultural and multireligious society.

When looking to when Western Christendom became a state religion in the fourth century during the Roman Empire and when the Western church got rigid hierarchical power structures, the prophetic identity of ecumenical stewardship does not seem to have had any major relevance for the church.[1] The Western pressure for expansion, growth, and power, where religion played a significant role, has had a strong impact on the universal spread of hierarchical and differentiated structures into the wider world.[2] The overall conclusion stated in all of the chapters is about an out-rationalization of social and moral responsibilities, the local community and the identity of the church as a sign of peace, justice, and unity. I have

---

1. Hall, *The Steward*; Bosch, *Transforming Mission*.
2. Scott, *Institutional Environments*.

also understood that much of the conflicts and differentiations in modern societies are due to the disintegrations between the modern and traditional cultures, represented by the profane and the sacred, the economy and faith, politics and religion, or development and mission. My overall conclusion on this is that the power of the West and impact of colonialism and globalization is a significant root cause of conflicts in the wider world. This leads to local and intercultural conflicts, competition for meager resources, and even terrorism. As I have stated elsewhere in this book, it is widely believed in the West that poverty and lack of development is a main root cause of conflict and violence in developing countries.

I would, however, say it is the power of the West and the elite groups in the rest of the world with pressure for further accumulation of wealth, economic growth, and expansions into new emerging markets that should be the main root cause for conflicts. What happens is that the belief in globalization, rationality, and modernization leads to neglect of social, spiritual, and cultural identities that are not so easy to measure and are not prioritized in global spirit for individualism and privatization. The power of the Western political and welfare institutions and business markets, which are being globalized in more or less the same way as some of the more progressive modern evangelical outreach missions from Western churches, create new sects that are supposed to compete for new customers and souls in order to accumulate necessary resources for their organizations.

In contrast to modern economics, capital growth, and competition for resources I have demonstrated how the stewardship philosophy as an economy of grace shifts emphasis to a more inclusive view, where spiritual, cultural, human, and natural resources are all seen as *gifts of grace* to be shared for the benefit of all people and for the generations to come. This perspective is also largely congruent with deeper understandings of social, economic, and ecological philosophies such as *oikonomia*, *oikoumene*, and *oikology*. A study of economic principles in some major traditional cultures and religions indicated they all, according to their faith and doctrines, underline the importance of mutual responsibility, economic justice, and peace in the world at large.

Concluding Analysis

In general, we can conclude that Western globalization, with the pressure for modernization and economic growth rooted in Western culture, leads to increasing institutional disintegrations, fragmentations, and conflicts that out-rationalize the common identity of peace, unity, and justice in the global household (*oikoumene*). What happens instead is a diversity of institutions and organizations with specific identities related to different cultures, traditions, and religions forms. It appears thus as a kind of continuation of the feudalistic type of power, with divide and rule, or what has been defined here as fragmented centralization. As the Western modern culture is rooted in the modern Enlightenment period since the seventeenth century, I conclude that the divisions, disintegrations, or conflicts that appear between traditional and modern identities may be rooted in a dualism between subjective and objective realities, an idea introduced by the French philosopher René Descartes. This explains the egocentric identity of the West, who sees the rest of the world as object for modernization, exploitation, and economic growth.

This has of course a profound impact on the Western church also. The wider impact of Western globalization, with its belief in modern rationality and institutionalization, is internal secularization with increasing business orientation of local congregations and the pressure for growth and progress in terms of membership and income.

Western secularization has also consequences for the separation of natural science from the science of humanities and religion, or the separation of spirit, humanity, and nature in general. The reference to God and religion in the West, which has been made by the State and in modern economics (the invisible hand of God), has been made in order to get popular support and legitimacy for power and the accumulation of wealth. Therefore, a major controversial issue is how the image of God is thought of, as it will have fundamental implications for the interpretation of power.

The general conclusions I have made leads to me to suggest the following hypotheses:

1. There is typical conflict between modern and traditional cultural identities, due to a Western and anthropocentric view of

the rest of the world as "undeveloped."

2. There is neglect of social, ethical, moral, and social values, which are difficult to measure due to modern pressure for measurability of effectiveness and progress, typical of Western globalization with its belief in economic rationality and progress.

3. The institutional structure of the Western church has differentiated into denominations, churches, and sects, which has been described as a fragmented centralization of power. This happened both in medieval times and as a result of modernization in the West with the emergence of modern national identities. This has also led to conflicts between the national government and the local ethnicities and religions outside the Western countries.

4. Disintegrations from the identity of a united church are rooted both in the Roman Empire and the Western belief in growth, rationality, and progress, and have led to a disintegration of overall identity into many different confessions, doctrines, and sectarian beliefs.

5. Western globalization has today implied a shift from politics to a market-oriented society, where the power of economic rationality dominates over social and ecological concerns.

6. The ecosophic stewardship model serves to explain in relative detail the strategies and moral principles of integration and allocation within a common identity of a multicultural economy grace, which is for the benefit of all in the global household.

7. The philosophy of ecological humanism has great potential to explain the interdependence of the sacred and profane institutional spheres of religion and economy. They are here seen as inter-subjective categories regardless of being in the West or East or modern and traditional cultures.

8. The concept of stewardship can be applied in the business society and public sector as well. The challenges of stewardship serve to integrate the wider social, cultural, and ecological demands over and above the demands for economic growth and the belief in rationality.

9. The production of goods and services for the benefit of the wider society should therefore have priority over profit-oriented purposes or to accumulate wealth for the owners. It is not a matter of self-interest only but for the benefit of an integrated global household.
10. The stewardship model helps integrate the diverse images of God or gods, which otherwise are referred to for the legitimacy of power over land and resources.

All of this will be further elaborated in this concluding analysis.

THE RELIGIOUS ROOTS OF DISINTEGRATION

The historical overview in the introduction indicated that the disintegration of a united church away from its original prophetic identity started right after the Early Christian period with the establishment of the church as a state religion in the fourth century by the Roman emperor Constantine I. Formal doctrines were agreed upon and enforced by the emperor, which eventually led to serious conflicts and wars with kingdoms in the Near East, where the Orthodox Church had been adopted as state religion. These wars weakened the Roman Empire and most of the Eastern kingdoms later fell into the hands of Arabs supported by the new religion of Islam.

This is of course not to say that there has been no prophetic witness since then. Many martyrs and prophets have suffered and contributed to the restoration of the original visions according to the identity of a united church. This happened many times during the Middle Ages, the Reformation period in the sixteenth century, and the Great Awakening in the nineteenth and twentieth centuries. It has happened both in the Eastern and Western churches and also in the South. However, this has not been the focus of this study, which has concentrated mainly on the institutional-cultural disintegration in Western churches and the impact from modern economic globalization.

What we can learn today from this is that conflicts and disintegration appear most often between secular authorities and

The Power of the West in the Economy of Grace

religious organizations, rather than between local communities of believers. Religion has even been used by political powers to legitimate war and power over resources. This of course raises questions about the image of God. The stewardship model and the identity of a prophetic church depart from the image of the body of Christ, rather than a super power that runs from the emperor or the king down to bishops and priests. I shall come back to this later in the concluding analysis. We can therefore assume it should probably be easier to discuss issues concerning the ecumenical stewardship of diverse talents and resources at local levels of society rather than at higher levels of religious authority.

My conclusion is therefore that a religious, traditional, and political image of a high God have been used to constitute the hierarchical structures in the society at large.

POWER IN THE IMAGE OF GOD

In the introduction, the identity of a prophetic church was explained in the image of the body of Christ in order to manifest peace, love, and unity. In the analysis, we have frequently observed that both political and religious authority structures have, however, received legitimacy and support with references to God.

The writers in the new institutionalism vein of research have also been clear that the Western globalization of institutional structures have been imposed from above. The Christian church and Christendom has played a significant role in the formation of "institutional structures constituting state, society and the individual" in what they call the "Western cultural account."[3]

In the chapter "Rationalizations of the Kingdom of God," I concluded that the disintegration into many different denominations with their specific doctrines and confessions depended on varying beliefs or interpretations of the kingdom of God. The power of the state needed support and legitimacy from a state religion or a national church, although there was little mutual understanding. In postmodern and secular society, the diversity of faiths and gods

3. Meyer, *Institutional Structure*, 12–37.

can perhaps also provide legitimacy for competing interests in a pluralistic society, although it rejects the belief in a God.

The challenge for a prophetic church is to adapt the institutional structures, the allocation of resources, etc., along the principles of a stewardship of grace, which is based on the identity of a prophetic church that emphasizes the equality of all, and not least the role of men and women.

Prophetic stewardship also implies living faith through deeds, which particularly stress mutual responsibility and sharing resources for the benefit of all. It would then stand in sharp contrast to the hierarchical power structures of the church, which have been institutionalized since the Constantine era in the fourth century. It is therefore not very strange that economic justice according to the stewardship idea has not always been taken seriously by the church.

THE PROPHETIC IDENTITY OF THE CHURCH AS A MORAL COMMUNITY

The overall conclusion I would draw from the analysis of Western globalization with institutionalization in Western churches in the preceding chapters is that the prophetic identity of the church as a sign of peace and unity in the world, has not been well recognized. This has been explained above as out-rationalization, which refers in particular to westernization of the institutional culture with its strong belief in rationality, competition, economic growth, and market expansion.

A vertical disintegration of structures concerns in particular a centralization of decision-making, where the united body of local congregations is being disengaged as a result of Western globalization. Horizontally, we have seen a disintegration of a united church body into different conflicting or competing beliefs with different doctrines, denominations, free churches, sects, etc. The processes of modernization and secularization in Western societies also create a typical differentiation between the spiritual and material aspects in modern society at large.

Institutional structures and economic systems in the multiplicity of denominations, movements, and sects do not clearly reflect any overall ecumenical identity in the image of the body of Christ. The institutional systems are universally standardized and often created in order to receive support and legitimacy for power from religion or the State. The impact from the globalization of market economics and the business culture with the pressure for privatization, growth, and competition seems now to increase over the legitimating role of the State in relation to the church. What then happens, for instance, is that churches are seen more as enterprises to be managed in a rational and economically efficient way rather than as a united body of local congregations, communities of believers who are signs of peace and unity.

One of the arguments for the disconnection between church identity and structure has been that the gospel is not concerned with organizational structures, which can be adapted to what may be seen as the most practical. In mainstream theological research in the West, it has commonly been argued that institutional structures, leadership styles, decision making, etc., of various churches and faith communities, have adapted to the specific local cultural context in the course of history. Unity in terms of doctrine and teaching the gospel should have been maintained through the apostolic succession of the highest religious authorities, from the first apostles to the popes, patriarchs, and bishops up until the present time.[4] The conclusion I have made is, however, that the structures of the Western church are not really based on the prophetic identity as a united church.

Matters of economic or ecological justice and other social or political matters of this world have also not had primary importance for the church. The Lutheran doctrine of two kingdoms has been used (perhaps misused) in order to defend the separation of the two governments over creation and salvation between the state and the church. This has, however, had the effect in that religion and politics are often separated in the Western church and Western theology has not concerned the institutional/cultural disintegration from the identity of the church.

---

4. Holmberg, *Paul and Power*; Dunn, *Unity and Diversity in the New Testament*.

Concluding Analysis

My conclusion from the above analysis is, however, that an ecumenical and ecosophic stewardship of grace suggests that a prophetic church today would need to engage seriously in the protests against social, economic, and ecological injustices as part of their mission.

THE PROPHETIC MISSION OF THE CHURCH

Already in the introductory chapters, it was made clear that the stewardship of the grace of God was the mission of the church. In the analysis above, I demonstrated however that the role of stewardship in Western society seems to have been out-rationalized in the institutional developments of foreign mission and aid organizations. This has of course also had a problematic impact on how the prophetic identity of the church's mission for peace and justice now seems to be out-rationalized.

From the analysis in the second chapter, I concluded that the institutionalization of national churches in East Africa in the twentieth century can be seen as rationalization of doctrines, confessions, national identities, strategies, and goals in Western churches. This happened in parallel to the political decolonization and the forming of modern nation states. There was further development into a multiplicity of projects that became financed by foreign aid from state aid agencies and church-related aid organizations.

The belief in modern rationality and progress with fragmentation of self-interest, project orientation, and competition for resources marginalized a local and united church body. The grants from Western mission organizations and churches often continued to earmark their grants to their mission fields. The project funding and earmarking of aid according to foreign preferences caused a fragmented centralization of power to central authorities of the church and particularly to foreign donors in the West. The secular development aid agencies in the West usually demand a separation of development projects away from local united church body. In many countries, this has led to dual structures: one for spiritual work and one for development, which does not reflect the holistic view that local churches in traditional cultures commonly maintain. This issue has also been the subject for many discussions, studies, and debate in partnership meetings. However, the project funding continues and leads to further fragmentation and detailed control, reports, and evaluations.

The consequence of this has been that it does not allow the local church to make its own priorities within an agreed and comprehensive budget approved by a united church body. And it does not allow the national church to exercise a wider and mutual responsibility where various other local, cultural, and human resources are being integrated for ecumenical stewardship within the church as a whole. What also happens is that conflicts and competition between various supporting partners and between local units of the united church develop in relation to fragmented funding. This is also commonly related to different local ethnicities, which then may lead to political conflicts.

The pressure for growth leads easily to the pressure for external funding from different foreign sources, which may not identify with a united church body and the local cultural context. The lack of a wider ecumenical identity as well as pressure for state aid among Western partners contributes thus to a marginalization of the local cultural context as well as disconnections from the overall prophetic identity of the church. Further, this external disintegration of funding as well as confessional divisions are related to the political disintegration and international conflicts on world community level.

What we can learn from this is that the Western globalization and anthropocentric worldview have also had an impact on the institutional development of mission and other church-related aid organizations in the West. Mission is now popularly understood as an enterprise into foreign countries mainly in the South and the East. Social development or aid is treated by secular and state agencies as a profane activity different from the main concern of the church.

The ecosophic worldview, however, helps us to see more clearly the interdependence between spirit, humanity, and nature, which promotes a sustainable and holistic mission. The sacred and profane activities in mission and development are interrelated and cannot really be structurally differentiated, without losing its prophetic identity as a stewardship of grace. Both mission and development are in fact modern concepts and reflect this Western culture of globalization and the belief in rationality. I would therefore suggest that the modern concepts of mission and development in the context of churches are replaced with the stewardship of grace or stewardship of peace, which covers both spiritual and material aspects.

ECUMENICAL IDENTITY

The doctrines and confessions of different denominations and faith communities often stress belief in Lutheran, Baptist, Pentecostal, Catholic, or Orthodox ideas. Our analysis tells us that different confessions and doctrines of faith and religious teaching can be seen as out-rationalizations of a common and overall identity. According to our analytical framework and to promote a prophetic church as a witness of unity and peace it should be necessary first to declare a common identity above the confessional identities for each faith community. The united church identity as a body of Christ is commonly manifested in, for instance, the Eucharist and regular preaching, but it is not much reflected in doctrinal, institutional, and strategic documents. It seems as if modern theology and the belief in rationality, science, and truth have had a strong impact on the formation of doctrines and the confessions of faith in modern churches.

When it comes to the ecumenical bodies of, for instance, the World Council of Churches and the Lutheran World Federation in Geneva, as well as Pentecostals, Catholics and Orthodox Churches, there are many challenges. Ecumenical as well as interreligious work should, according to the stewardship model, promote cooperation and the manifestation of unity based on the common identity of a body of God and the economy of grace. This means that each faith community, church, and religion primarily manifests a common identity in the image of God and demonstrates peace and fair sharing of resources for the benefit of all.

The specific confessions of each can easily disregard the common prophetic and moral message of being together in solidarity, including the issue of grace, that is, the love and mercy from God also in organizational documents and doctrines. My conclusion is that an economy of grace with ecumenical stewardship will have to also be highlighted in doctrines and strategic documents.

The challenge of stewardship, based on the identity of the church as a body of Christ, therefore has great potential to promote mutual responsibility across denominational boundaries. Churches at large often keep two separate tracks, one for religion and another for worldly activities. The stewardship principles based on the image of a body of Christ would enforce a horizontal integration or at least mutual responsibility and interdependence between the church work and the development projects. Also, the political sphere strives to keep religion separate from politics. There is then a great risk that religious fundamentalism or rationalism will increase as a reaction to increasing secularization in the society at large. Also here the stewardship model of leadership and organization will strengthen the unity of the church and see the gospel of grace to include social, political, and economic justice as well.

IDENTITY AND STRUCTURES

The challenge of stewardship and the ecosophic worldview, which has been raised against modernization from the Western and anthropocentric worldview, should thus also have an impact on the theology of the church (ecclesiology), that has been developed since the Enlightenment. This concerns particularly issues of leadership, society, politics, ecology, and economy. Church institutions should thus reflect peace and unity in the ecumenical identity of a prophetic church. The main reason is that political or secular structures and economy are not neutral or objective categories, but are injected with culture and norms.

The postmodern culture of increasing fragmentation and market competition has implied more religious enterprises and sects based on a multiplicity of religious beliefs, and has in fact worsened the problems of disintegration and disunity. The stewardship mystery of grace is, however, not accepted in the postmodern view of pluralism and relativism, where competition between spiritual experiences and religious multiplicity would be seen as a resource. It would just be one of many models of interpretation, and therefore it risks being out-rationalized.

The mystery of grace is expressed in poetic and symbolic language, and then interpreted in a modern and scientific context. Our analytical model is based on this mystery and does not therefore exist empirically. It is not possible to make any rational observation in order to locate it. The mystery of grace in the Bible is presented almost entirely in parables and was also difficult to control during early period of Christianity.

Organizational, leadership and economic studies of the church should therefore treat identity and structure as interdependent. The church as a whole could thus be treated as a sacrament, the image of the body of Christ. Therefore, power structures or the sharing resources should ideally reflect this prophetic image or symbol. A prophetic stewardship implies commitment to radical positions on issues of peace and justice including cultural, economic, and ecological concerns as well.

Above all the church needs to reflect further on the image of God, and the role of secularization as well, which seems to have developed in relation to the secular power of the state and the church. Alternative images could be to see the kingdom of God as a symbol of grace, unity, love, or peace rather than being linked with the Western culture of Christendom or the institutional spheres of the church. To promote a united and prophetic church the diversity of church denominations and doctrines would therefore have to see their respective doctrine or creed within the wider ecumenical identity or the united image of the universal church as a sacrament (sign of grace) of the body of Christ. What seems to have happened, however, is that this image has been largely left out in the Western churches and, to a certain extent, replaced with the specific confessions of the various denominations. It is however more visible in the Orthodox Church and some of the ecumenical bodies.

The Power of the West in the Economy of Grace

INTERRELATIONS OF RELIGION AND ECONOMY

I concluded above that religious belief might sometimes be used by business to get legitimacy for economic progress and capitalism. On the other hand business-oriented entrepreneurship, market orientation, or growth and prosperity may also be used by religion to get legitimacy and support from members or the business market. Competition among faith communities with different confessions, and production of religious service may then develop. The impact from globalization seems then to have an impact on modern religion, which is an indication that postmodern religion derives its legitimacy from the free market rather than from the State.

The modern and free churches get legitimacy for being a charismatic, effective, and living church as they adopt modern entrepreneurial and popular models of management from the business market and modern education. In the new churches, the identity of a prophetic church is out-rationalized when institutional systems are now adopted from the business market rather than from the State.

What should be necessary, if departing from the ecosophic worldview, is to develop models of leadership and structures, which are based on common identity of the church as a whole, including organization and economy. Church and theology still has important knowledge, which can also contribute to a sustainable society, as well as to the formation of economic systems and leadership. On the other hand, church and religion has an obligation to listen to other disciplines than theology such as sociology; and, of course, to include church politics, organization, or economy so as to learn from theology.

I would also conclude that the legitimating of business capitalism and economic growth with self-interest, and the invisible hand of God according to Adam Smith, might be seen as a rationalization of faith. The modern and rationalized economic systems with self-interested competition that we face today contribute, however, to an increasing economic injustice, social misery, and ecological threats, which is rather contradictory to faith in peace and justice.

The stewardship model based on the ecosophic worldview would therefore contribute to mutual responsibility between the religious and the secular in order to commonly stress the humanitarian, social, or ecological threats.

STEWARDSHIP IN THE SEARCH FOR INTERRELIGIOUS IDENTITY

In the chapter about a multicultural and global economy including different cultures and religions, I concluded that all traditional cultures and religions seemed to refer to economic principles similar to the stewardship model. The ideal was sharing resources for the benefit of all and an emphasis on social integration that somehow was rather different from the Western and modern view of economics. The modern understanding of economic rationality was disintegrated from the local cultural identity and the management was narrowed down to mainly financial and other measurable categories.

Ecumenical stewardship with an ecosophic worldview should therefore be one useful basis for interreligious peace and identity. As we have seen throughout religious history, there have been war and conflicts. Today peace and justice is severely threatened not least in Western societies with conflicts between religious/traditional rationalism and modern rationalism with its strong belief in secularism and science.

The stewardship principle departs from a vision of a prophetic church of peace, love, and unity. Therefore, the church and religion has a prophetic role to play in the vision for peace in the world. Stewardship means in particular that churches and also religions have to be visible signs of unity in order for the rest of society to follow the same path.

In the following I will demonstrate how the stewardship idea with an ecosophic worldview can serve as a basis for a transformation of Western and modern institutional cultures and principles. It concerns both power and ethics of economy, leadership, and organization.

The Power of the West in the Economy of Grace

THE GLOBALIZATION OF WESTERN ECONOMICS

The critique raised against modern economic systems ended in suggestions for transfigurations into new economic or financial systems without radical changes in worldviews. The ecosophic worldview departs however from the view that there is an interdependence of humanity, spirit, and nature. We have however, to realize that the present economic systems are typically narrow in technical and material terms. They are even part of the wider institutional culture and rationality that is characteristic of the Western anthropocentric view as it was described in the introduction. The most important conclusion concerning the critique against this is thus that the same structures and processes are being adopted almost all over the world. The new institutional theories explained it as a "rationalization of the resource environment"[5] due to the dependence on Western modernization. Churches are also adopting them without realizing that they carry with them values and cultures that are not socially or culturally embedded or rooted in the identity of the church.[6]

We also concluded in the preceding chapters about the role of the church in development, that various organizational and economic systems and structures in Africa have been instituted as a rationalization of the goals and preferences of Western mission and aid organizations, particularly state aid agencies extending aid for national development and modernization.

The general critique raised against modern economics is thus rooted in the belief in modernity and progress with its anthropocentric worldview, where the Western civilization is often assumed to be the subject in the center of world development, and the rest of the world and natural resources are treated as objects to be explored for continued growth and development. This colonialization has created a lot of conflicts and violence. The South is misrepresented in the global household, where social, economic, and ecological justice should be necessary for a sustainable society.

---

5. Scott, *Institutional Environments*, 28.
6. Giddens, *The Consequences of Modernity*.

Concluding Analysis

It is from this Western anthropocentric view, including religion as well as politics, we have to understand the creation of the universal institutional systems applied almost universally due to the impact of globalization.

ETHICS AND ECONOMY

In chapter 3, I outlined some of the most controversial issues within business and politics regarding the dilemma between ethics and economy. The conclusion I want to make here is that the increasing pressure for economic growth in the West leads to the disregard of social responsibility and ecological debts, both towards exploited human and natural resources in the East and South. The pressure for economic growth in the European Economic Community, for instance, has further implied huge national debts to be paid by coming generations in order to get access to natural resources in the East. It has also implied huge national debts for the US, due to heavy military budgets and wars in Iraq and Afghanistan. Also, these debts are for the coming generations to pay. This can be seen as out-rationalizations of a moral community, which has no voice in a market economy.

The overall welfare of society is subject to widespread rationalizations using statistics of GNP (Gross National Products), which, however, do not measure human, cultural, and spiritual resources that are being consumed in the process, let alone the destruction of huge human resources and welfare investments due to the heavy investments in war expenditures. Also ecological threats and attempts to save the climate are measured in statistical figures such as emission rights in order to pay for our ecological debts. This is therefore to be seen as an out-rationalization of the moral impulse.

The social and ecological responsibility of business corporations is difficult to maintain in a market economy where business depends on the competitive power in order to stay in business.

However, the business depends also on social legitimacy from the staff, media, and community. Therefore, it is doing a lot in order to market an image of a Corporate Social Responsibility (CSR), particularly when it is believed to increase the market shares due to the publicity.

My conclusion is that the overall identity and purpose of business should be to produce social welfare, mutual responsibility, and benefit for all in principally the same way as for society as a whole. What has happened, however, is that this overall identity and purpose has been rationalized or narrowed down to financial self-interests in order to accumulate wealth for the owners.

It has been taken for granted that the role of business is to make profits, but why should business not have an overall purpose to produce goods and services for the benefit of welfare for all? This should be particularly important at this time with various threats against a sustainable world. They can, with the theory of competitive advantage and mutual responsibility and cooperation, develop their particular knowledge and expertise in the production of goods and services to promote both welfare and social responsibility. Monetary profit is received as a result and the condition for long-term economic sustainability, rather than having it as the overall goal. If profit maximization were the goal, it would receive legitimacy even for the production of goods, which are not socially sustainable. Thus, the purpose of welfare for all and business ethics is out-rationalized.

AN ECO-SOPHIC ECONOMY

Based on the brief review of the beliefs of the economic principles of major religions and cultures, I have concluded that the classical model of stewardship and the economy of grace outlined in the introduction could serve as a basis for the development of an ecosophic economy where different cultures are seen as resources rather than as constraints. It should also open up for a new relation to Eastern churches and religions. It recognizes in particular the specific and unique resources, gifts, and talents given to each person as well as each culture and religion for the benefit of all.

It may be unrealistic to think the world as a whole would be able to agree on a common new economic system as has been commonly suggested in the critique. So far, all the ecumenical endeavors in history have concerned conflicts between different doctrines and between different religious authorities, views, and interests, while the local churches and communities have not been much involved. So in the struggle for unity they have largely been left out, which reminds us of the powerful Western anthropocentric and hierarchical worldview.

We can still conclude that all related faith communities in their teaching see the economic core principles as a divine household economy, stressing mutual responsibility and sharing for the benefit of all, similar to the stewardship perspective outlined above. Properties are in principle given by God, and should therefore not be reserved only for the accumulation of private resources. There is wider mutual responsibility and accountability for the stewardship of all resources given (human, spiritual, or natural). Consequently, it rejects both a rationalistic interpretation of state economy or market economy. Both of these are rooted in the Western and modern anthropocentric paradigm and based on self-interested rationality. They must both be governed by mutual responsibility and accountability with a fair stewardship of resources between all people in the world. The present system of capital interest in Western economy is therefore questionable, if it is not shared for a wider benefit of others.

With the stewardship principle of mutual responsibility there is shared risk between the loan taker and the lender (for instance, in Islamic economics), which considerably reduces the need for high interest. Western economic rationalities, where all risks are rationalized into interest to be paid by the loan taker, lead to a greater risk for increasing prices on properties and the increasing risk taken by the banks.

STEWARDSHIP AND THE ROLE OF WOMEN

As I mentioned above regarding the anthropocentric worldview, I concluded that the almost powerless role of women through church history, and also in society at large, is an important explanatory factor for the structural disintegration and out-rationalization of a prophetic and united church body. In my studies of church structures and the problems of fragmentation and conflicts, men have played the most powerful role.

The principles of stewardship and the ecosophic worldview would, however, be far more suitable for equality between men and women. It has also been my experience, from work in Africa in particular, that women are far more interested in the ideas of stewardship and mutual responsibility. Stewardship underlines that both genders have an important role to play with their unique gifts. Equality is necessary for the sake of integration and unity as well as efficiency and growth.

The role of women in leadership is more integrative, social, and relational than what is usually shown in the role of men's leadership, who may press more for short-term efficiency and profit orientation.

STEWARDSHIP FOR A CORPORATE SOCIAL RESPONSIBILITY

Tradition as well as modernity has been characterized by hierarchical or top-down structures of bureaucracy and goal-oriented rationalities and control, which do not recognize the need for mutual responsibility in line with the ecosophic worldview. The Western organizational systems are also typically disembodied from the social context as well as local or global household principles, which make it difficult to integrate various resources, as it was outlined in the stewardship model and the economy of grace. The many popular models of management, servant-oriented leadership, bottom up, local empowerment, entrepreneurship etc., are, however, not commonly assuming any ecosophic worldview as it was described at the beginning. This should make any changes in styles of leadership or any new economic order rather ineffective if not unrealistic.

The stewardship principle suggested would instead encourage a leadership that assumes mutual responsibility between people at large and also between various section leaders, rather than running

Concluding Analysis

from the top. Such a model of leadership would also be suitable for corporations working together in a network of relations.

What relevance does this now have for other organizations and business corporations? The most obvious conclusion I would draw is that the identity and purpose of business to produce goods and services for the benefit of all have been, in new modern economics, rationalized into the purpose of making profit for the interest of the owners mainly. Therefore, organizations may be identified as profit and non-profit organizations, rather than serving a wider social purpose. Monetary profit is the goal rather than the result of the business activities. Even privately owned social sector organizations are run as profit making entities. Here it should be obvious that there is a social purpose although profit will be a condition or a result of activities in the longer term.

In all of these organizations or corporations, there is a challenge of stewardship. In a similar way as the church, other corporations (lat. corpus=body) could also be seen as having a particular role to provide necessary goods and services for the benefit of all. The stewardship view also respects the tradition social embeddedness, which also helps promote a corporate social responsibility (CSR). Each person is created with a unique gift and with unique competence. Together in a corporation or in a network of corporate bodies one can also talk about a stewardship of a variety of talents, gifts, and resources working with mutual responsibility. This is different from the model of management, which normally implies the setting of goals and an efficient control of operations directed from the owners or from the managing director in order to maximize the profit for the owners. With the ecosophic worldview, we can further underline a social, spiritual, economic, and ecological sustainability, which is not assumed in the modern management model.

STEWARDSHIP OF INTERNATIONAL AID

In the discussion on development aid in the introductory chapters, we saw the risk for fragmented centralization through the institutionalization of projects. There is, of course, also a risk for poor stewardship of aid that is given towards an annual budget if there is little control. My conclusion here is, of course, that all receivers and givers have a mutual responsibility and accountability for all resources given. This is particularly so as none of them can treat the gifts as privately owned, as they in principle are given by grace.

Therefore, the aid to poor people together with other income should be accounted for through annual reports and evaluations. These should be provided openly to local communities as well as to foreign supporters. A mutual accountability also implies that the income of the aid giver and the dispensation of aid should also be shown in a transparent way. This is the kind of stewardship that is necessary in order to avoid corruption and misuse of all resources.

What has instead usually been demanded is the reduction of foreign aid in favor of business or only aid that is designated for particular purposes that would also benefit the aid giver.

My conclusion from the discussion above is that it would not strengthen the need for mutual responsibility and fair and democratic stewardship of the aid. The stewardship must also be locally integrated so as to be transparent for the wider community and induce local support.

STEWARDSHIP OF LOCAL RESOURCES IN THE MAINTENANCE OF PEACE

We concluded in the discussion of stewardship for peace that modern peacemaking has focused more on managing conflicts than the maintenance of peace and preventing conflict. The stewardship approach assumes peace is a resource that needs to be cared for. Conflict management is more of a curative approach, which of course is necessary in the short term. To maintain peace and unity in the long run it is therefore necessary to examine the root causes of conflicts related to human resources and local traditional cultures.

We have already seen from the history of the institutional development of churches that conflicts have been related to the structural differentiation, competition for resources and doctrinal differences at higher institutional levels, but they are also related to competition for material resources and power. Justice and equality is therefore necessary in order to prevent conflict and maintain peace. This includes, of course, equality between men and women.

A stewardship of peace and unity needs to involve human and cultural resources that may not be included in the modern institutional systems. A major resource is all the people who have retired or who have immigrated and are well educated and experienced, but are not contributing to peace and development. They may even get social aid but are not given much opportunity to contribute their skills as they have been out-rationalized in the traditional cultural context. With a stewardship approach to economic thinking, one would treat such resources as expenditure if it were not utilized.

In a similar way, it would be more important to reduce income tax for educated youth and the jobless rather than reduce tax for people who work fulltime. With a stewardship approach to the economy the cultural and spiritual resources would be valued higher, as well as the voluntary work in non-profit organizations and the role of women in peacemaking.

STEWARDSHIP OF NATURE

With a stewardship approach, all natural resources are treated as gifts received by grace. Nobody has paid anything to nature for the ecosystem, which provides a lot of energy, and which is the real source of all growth and development. What we pay for is the exploration of it but not the resource itself, of course. The present threat against the climate, which is caused primarily by Western civilization, has caused severe damages to other civilizations in the East and the South. And it has been particularly the poor who are suffering from desertification, floods, and drought. Consequently, there is a huge ecological debt caused by the Western and anthropocentric worldview. With an ecosophic worldview and the ecumenical stewardship principle in the global household the demand for eco-justice will become a great challenge.

The Power of the West in the Economy of Grace

THE MYSTERY OF THE ECONOMY OF GRACE

Right from the beginning, we have seen that there is a typical dualism between sacredness and economy, religious and secular, identity and structure, grace and law, tradition and modernity, integration and disintegration, subject and object, unity and diversity, faith and reason, socialism and individualism, and much more. This has also characterized the emergence of the division between the East and West. My conclusion is therefore that this dualism may also be the source for institutional disintegration, injustice, and conflicts in the world.

Instead, the ecosophic worldview and the economy of grace direct attention to an invisible God who is the owner and root source of grace. This was also in the mind of Adam Smith who referred to the "invisible hand of God," and also Linnaeus who saw the "back" of God in the Nature. The institutional structures and economic systems of Western society lead us, on the other hand, to the public image of a high God above it all and outside the world, who then gives legitimacy to hierarchical structures as well as belief in rationality, growth, welfare, and expansion of an earthly prosperity, or the kingdom of God. We can therefore see the hierarchical structures of power as rationalization of such an image of God. The pluralistic and postmodern view of culture and religion lead us to an individualistic image of different gods. This corresponds to the market view of religion, where different faith communities compete with a diversity of spiritual services according to demand from the members.

The ecosophic view and the stewardship philosophy of mutual responsibility would instead lead us nearer to the mystery of the economy of grace that is present in nature, humanity, and spirit for the benefit of all. These three can be seen as gifts received for the benefit of all, and as three aspects resembling the image of the body of God in the Trinity.

Bibliography

Asseffa, Hizkias. "Critical Perspectives on Theory and Practice of Peace Paper presented at Tools for Peace Consultation." Life and Peace Institute, Uppsala, 2003.
Atherton, John. *Transfiguring Capitalism: An Enquiry into Religion and Global Change.* London: SCM Press, 2008.
Bateson, Gregory. *A Sacred Unity: Further Steps to an Ecology of Mind.* Edited by Rodney E. Donaldson. New York: HarperCollins, 1991.
Baumann, Zygmunt. *Postmodern Ethics.* Oxford: Blackwell Publishers, 1993.
Berg, Aart Nicolaas van den. *God and the Economy: Theological Documents on the Economy.* Delft, Netherlands: Eburon, 1998.
Berger, Peter, and Thomas Luckmann. *The Social Construction of Reality: A Treatise in the Sociology of Knowledge.* Garden City, NJ: Double Day, 1966.
Bergeron, Suzanne. "Political Economy Discourses of Globalization and Feminist Politics." *Signs* 26 (2001) 983–1006.
Berry, R. J. *God's Book of Works: The Nature and Theology of Nature.* New York: Templeton Press, 2003.
Beyer, Peter. *Religion and Globalization.* Sage Publications: London, 1994.
Boraks, Lucius. *Religions of the West.* Kansas City: Rowman and Littlefield, 1988.
Bosch, David Jacobus. *Transforming Mission: Paradigm Shifts in Theology of Mission.* Mary Knoll, NY: Orbis, 1992.
Brander, Bo. *Människan och den ekologiska väven.* Artos: Skellefteå, 2002.
Brattgård, Helge. *God's Stewards: A Theological Study of the Principles and Practices of Stewardship.* Translated by Gene J. Lund. Minneapolis: Augsburg, 1963.
Brodd, Sven-Erik. "Stewardship and Ecclesiology." In *Stewardship: Our Accountability to God.* Number 34. Geneva: Lutheran World Federation, 1994.
Carroll, Archie B. *Business and Society: Ethics and Stakeholder Management.* Mason, OH: South Western Cengage Learning, 2008.
Chaves, Mark. "Intraorganizational Power and Internal Secularization in Protestant Denominations." *American Journal of Sociology* 99:1 (1993) 1–48.

Bibliography

Chestnut, Andrew R. *Competitive Spirits: Latin America's New Religious Economy.* New York: Oxford University Press, 2003.

D'Costa, Gavin, editor. "Christ the Trinity and Religious Plurality." In *Christian Uniqueness Reconsidered: The Myth of a Pluralistic Theology of Religions.* Maryknoll, NY: Orbis, 1996.

Davies, Grace. *Religion in Modern Europe: A Memory Mutates.* European Societies. New York: Oxford University Press, 2000.

Davis, James H. "Toward a Stewardship Theory of Management." *Academy of Management Review* 22:1 (1997) 20–47.

Demerath, N. J. *Sacred Companies: Organizational Aspects of Religion and Religious Aspects of Organizations.* New York: Oxford University Press, 1998.

Duchrow, Ulrich, editor. *Faith Communities and Social Movements Facing Globalization.* International and Interfaith Colloquim 2000 on Faith-Theology Economy. Geneva: World Alliance of Reformed Churches, 2002.

Dunn, James D. G. *Unity and Diversity in the New Testament: An Inquiry into the Character of Earliest Christianity.* London: SCM Press, 2006.

Fehr, Ernst, et al. "'Economic Man' in Cross-Cultural Perspective: Behavioral Experiments in 15 Small-Scale Societies." *Behavioral and Brain Sciences* 28:6 (December 2005) 795–855.

Friedman, Milton. "The Social Responsibility of Business is to Increase Its Profits." *New York Times Magazine* (September 13, 1970).

Giddens, Anthony. *The Consequences of Modernity.* Stanford, CA: Stanford University Press, 1990.

Godlas, Alan. "Sufism, Sufists—Sufist Orders." Paper presented at University of Georgia, Athens, GA, 2001.

Grenholm, Carl-Henric, and Normunds Kamergrauzis, editors. *Sustainable Development and Global Ethics.* Uppsala Studies in Social Ethics. Stockholm: Uppsala universitat, 2007.

Hall, Douglas John. *The Steward: A Biblical Symbol Come of Age.* Grand Rapids: Eerdmanns, 1990.

Hallman, David G., editor. *Ecotheology: Voices from South and North.* Marknoll, NY: Orbis, 1994.

Hammarskjöld, Dag. *Markings.* Translated by Leif Sjöberg and W. H. Auden. New York: Ballantine Books, 1964.

Havnevik, Kjell, Tekeste Negash, and Atakilte Beyene. *Of Global Concern: Rural Livelihood Dynamics and Natural Resource Governance.* Sida Studies 6. Stockholm: Sida, 2006.

Holmberg, Bengt. *Paul and Power: The Structure of Authority in the Primitive Church as Reflected in the Pauline Epistles.* Lund: Gleerup, 1978.

Huntington, Samuel P. *The Clash of Civilizations and the Remaking of World Order.* New York: Simon and Schuster, 2011.

Jonsson, Eskil. *Att vara eller inte vara kyrka: Ett förvaltarskapsperspektiv.* SMR och LPI, 2002.

Bibliography

———. "Bistånd hotar kyrkans trovärdighet." In *Svensk Kyrkotidning*, 19–20. Stockholm: 2007.
———. *Narrow Management: The Quest for Unity in Diversity*. Uppsala: Lambert Academic, 1998.
Klein, Naomi. *The Shock Doctrine: The Rise of Disaster Capitalism*. London: Allen Lane, 2007.
Korten, David C. *Alternatives to Economic Globalization: A Better World is Possible*. San Francisco: Berrett-Koehler, 2004.
———. *The Post-Corporate World: Life After Capitalism*. San Francisco: Berrett-Koehler, 1999.
———. *When Corporations Rule the World*. San Francisco: Berrett-Koehler, 1995.
Kotler, Philip, and Nancy Lee. *Corporate Social Responsibility. Doing the Most Good for Your Company and Your Cause*. Hoboken, NJ: Wiley and Sons, 2005.
Labévière, Richard. *Dollars for Terror: The United States and Islam*. New York: Algora, 2000.
Lindskoug, Kerstin. *Hänförelse och förnuft, Om karisma och rationalitet i Max Webers sociologi*. Lund: Dialog, 1979.
Long, Stephen D. *Divine Economy: Theology and the Market*. New York: Routledge, 2000.
Lyotard, Jean François. *The Postmodern Condition: A Report on Knowledge*. Minneapolis: University of Minnesota Press, 1984.
LPI. "Papers and Presentations at 'Tools for Peace,' International Consultation October 2003." *New Routes* 8:3–4 (2003).
McFague, Sallie. *Models of God: Theology for an Ecological, Nuclear Age*. Philadelphia: Fortress Press, 1987.
Meeks, Douglas M. *God the Economist: The Doctrine of God and Political Economy*. Minneapolis: Fortress Press, 1989.
Meyer, John W., and Brian Rowan. "Institutionalized Organizations: Formal Structure as Myth and Ceremony." *American Journal of Sociology* 83:2 (1977) 340–63.
Meyer, John W., et al. *Institutional Structure: Constituting State, Society, and the Individual*. Newbury Park, CA: Sage, 1987.
Mudge, Lewis S. *The Church as a Moral Community: Ecclesiology and Ethics in Ecumenical Debate*. New York: Continuum, 1998.
Næss, Arne. *Ecology, Community, and Lifestyle: Outline of an Ecosophy*. New York: Cambridge University Press, 1989.
Nelson, Julie A. *Economics for Humans*. Chicago: University of Chicago Press, 2006.
Nelson, Robert. *Economics as Religion: From Samuelson to Chicago and Beyond*. Philadelphia: Pennsylvania State University Press, 2001.
O'Dea, Thomas F. "Five Dilemmas in the Institutionalization of Religion." *Journal for the Scientific Study of Religion* 1 (1961) 30–41.

Bibliography

OECD. *The Paris Declaration on Aid Effectiveness and Accra Agenda for Action.* OECD: Paris, 2005.

Ostrom, Elinor. *Governing the Commons: The Evolution of Institutions for Collective Action.* New York: Cambridge University Press, 1990.

Polanyi, Karl. *The Great Transformation: The Political and Economic Origins of Our Time.* Boston: Beacon Press, 2001.

Pfaffenholz, Thania. *Community Based Peace Building.* Uppsala: Life Peace Institute, 2007.

Purser, Ronald E., Changkil Park, and Alfonso Montuori. "Limits to Anthropocentrism: Toward an Ecocentric Organization Paradigm?" *Academy of Management Review* 20:4 (1995) 1053–89.

Reumann, John Henry Paul. *Stewardship and the Economy of God.* Grand Rapids: Eerdmans, 1992.

Rausing, L. "Underwriting the Oeconomy: Linneaus on Nature and Mind." *History of Political Economy* 35 (2003) pp 173–203.

Ray, Darby Kathleen, editor. *Theology that Matters: Ecology, Economy and God.* Minneapolis: Fortress Press, 2006.

Rosser, J. Barkley Jr., Kirby L. Kramer Jr., and Marina V. Rosser. "The New Traditional Economy: A New Perspective for Comparative Economics." *International Journal of Social Economics* 26:6 (1998) 763–78.

Scott, Richard W. *Institutional Environments and Organizations: Structural Complexity and Individualism.* Thousand Oaks, CA: SAGE, 1994.

Sen, Amartya. *On Ethics and Economics.* New York: Blackwell, 1992.

Skolimowski, Henryk. *Ecological Humanism.* Ann Arbor: Gryphon, 1975.

———. *A Sacred Place to Dwell: Living with Reverence upon the Earth.* Rockport, MA: Element Books, 1993.

Soderbaum, Peter. *Understanding Sustainability Economics. Towards Pluralism in Economics.* London: Routledge, 2008.

Stählin, Wilhelm. *Mysteriet, En bok om Guds hemligheter.* Stockholm: Verbum, 1994.

Stieglitz, Joseph. *Wither Socialism?* Cambridge, MA: MIT Press, 1994.

Tanner, Kathryn. *Economy of Grace.* Minneapolis: Fortress Press, 2005.

Thung, Mady A. *The Precarious Organisation: Sociological Explorations of the Church´s Mission and Structure.* Berlin: de Gruyter, 1976.

Tillard, Jean Marie Roger. *Church of Churches: The Ecclesiology of Communion.* Collegeville, MN: Liturgical, 1992.

Villa-Vicencio, Charles. *The Art of Reconciliation.* The Institute for Justice and Reconciliation. Berlin: de Gruyter, 1976.

Wall, Derek. *The Rise of the Green Left: Inside the Worldwide Ecosocialist Movement.* New York: Pluto, 2010.

Warner, R. Stephen. "Work in Progress toward a New Paradigm for the Sociological Study of Religion in the United States." *American Journal of Sociology* 98:5 (March 1993) 1044–93.

Bibliography

Weber, Max. *Economy and Society: An Outline of Interpretative Sociology.* Edited by Guenther Roth and Claus Wittisch. Berkeley, CA: University of California Press, 1968.

———. *The Protestant Ethic and the Spirit of Capitalism.* New York: Norton, 2009.

Wilber, Ken. *The Holographic Paradigm and Other Paradoxes: Exploring the Leading Edge of Science.* Boulder: Shambhala, 1982.

Wilson, Rodney. *Economics, Ethics and Religion: Jewish, Christian, and Muslim Economic Thought.* London: Macmillan, 1997.

Windell, Karolina. *Corporate Social Responsibility under Construction.* Företagsekonomiska Institutionen. Uppsala: Uppsala Universitet, 2006.

Woodhead, Linda, and Paul Heelas, editors. *Religion in Modern Times: An Interpretive Anthology.* Oxford, UK: Blackwell, 2000.

World Commission on Environment and Development. *Our Common Future.* New York: Oxford University Press, 1987.

www.ingramcontent.com/pod-product-compliance
Lightning Source LLC
Chambersburg PA
CBHW072149160426
43197CB00012B/2303